HOW To WOW

With PowerPoint

Richard Harrington & Scott Rekdal
RHED Pixel

Series Editor Jack Davis

Peachpit Press

How to Wow with PowerPoint
Richard Harrington and Scott Rekdal, RHED Pixel

Peachpit Press
1249 Eighth Street
Berkeley, CA 94710
510/524-2178
800/283-9444
510/524-2221 (fax)

Find us on the Web at: www.peachpit.com
To report errors, please send a note to errata@peachpit.com

Peachpit Press is a division of Pearson Education

Project Editor: Susan Rimerman
Production Editor: Hilal Sala
Copyeditor: Elaine Merrill
Indexer: Patti Schiendelman
Composition: David Van Ness
Cover Design: Jack Davis
Cover Production: Andreas Schueller
Interior Design: Jill Davis

ISBN 0-321-49573-X

9 8 7 6 5 4 3 2 1

Printed and bound in the United States of America

Dedications

To my wife, Meghan, thank you for your patience and love. To my son, Michael, you inspire me to be a better man. To my family, thank you for your guidance and support.

—Rich

To my amazing wife and best friend, Stefanie, thank you for your love and support. To my boys, Ryan and Tyler, thank you for the daily joy you bring me. To Mom and Dad, your love and support make anything possible.

—Scott

Image Acknowledgments

To those great folks who contributed real images and media to the book:

Chapter 1—National Science Foundation.

Individual photographers: Brien Barnett, Rhys Boulton, Chad Carpenter, Steve Clabuesch, Alexander Colhoun, Jack Cummings, Zee Evans, Glenn E. Grant, Patrick Hovey, Kristan Hutchison, Rob Jones, Jeffrey Kietzmann, Kris Kuenning, Levi Littrell, Ariana Owens, Steven Profaizer, Jaime Ramos, Peter Rejcek, Rebecca Shoop, Scott Smith, Peter Somers, Emily Stone, and Joe Tarnow.

Chapter 4—Amplifico (www.amplifico.net). If you are a music lover, go check them out (and buy a CD).

Acknowledgments

First, a big thank you to Scott, my co-author. His skills as an Art Director as well as his deep commitment to this project have made this book a true joy to work on. Our challenge was to take art-school techniques and translate them to the world of business communication, and I think we've succeeded.

To my friends, family, and colleagues who have served as a soundboard for this project, thank you! Tackling a topic that has been written about for years required fresh ideas and a new approach. Thank you for airing your frustrations with the status quo as well as for sharing your presentations for us to study, critique, and rebuild.

To my wife and son, thank you for keeping me company. I still don't know why I do my best writing at 2:00 a.m., but I'll work on that. Michael, your smiles mean the world; I always have time for you. To my wife: with all that you do, it's amazing that you have any patience left. Thank you for your understanding and support through this challenging project. Thank you for sticking with me and helping me laugh.

—Rich

First of all, I'd like to say thanks to Rich Harrington. If you drew a Venn diagram of proficiency in technology, creativity, and business, very few people would fit solidly in even two of those categories. Rich fits directly in the center of all three. You Rock!

Thanks to everyone who supported and inspired me. Thanks to: Jim Matejka for giving me my first ad agency job in New York; Bob Rainford and Debbie Frushour for 10 great years; Richard Tsai, Jerel Motos, and Charlie Schulze for inspiring me; Scott Bryant for your amazing creativity; Jeff Fisher and Owen Burns for accepting calls from Benjamin Kenobi; and John Suszczynski and Dean Pellerzi for your friendship and support.

Finally, I'd like to thank the real core team. To my wife, who has been by my side since we were teenagers—you've supported me through a career of all-nighters and caffeine binges and you've always been my foundation and my world. Thanks to my wonderful boys, Ryan and Tyler, for understanding when Daddy was "playing on the computer" in the office until all hours of the night.

—Scott

A big thanks to Jack Davis for creating such a great series of books. To Rebecca Gulick, thanks for thinking of us and giving us the chance. To Susan Rimerman, our editor, you kept us on track and polished our ideas to create a fantastic book. To the entire Peachpit team, your professional handling of this project continues to be always appreciated.

To all the great folks at RHED Pixel, who checked our work and picked up our slack, thank you.

To all the clients through the years who have challenged us, thank you for asking for more and never accepting the first draft "as-is."

To the Microsoft Office team, thanks for the fresh ideas and new tools. Keep pushing the program and giving communication pros more options.

To you, the reader, thanks for your support. We hope you enjoy this book and we welcome your feedback. Feel free to visit our resource blog at www.rastervector.com.

—Rich and Scott

Contents

6 ADDING MOTION & CREATIVE TRANSITIONS 142

7 DELIVERING THE PRESENTATION 160

Introduction

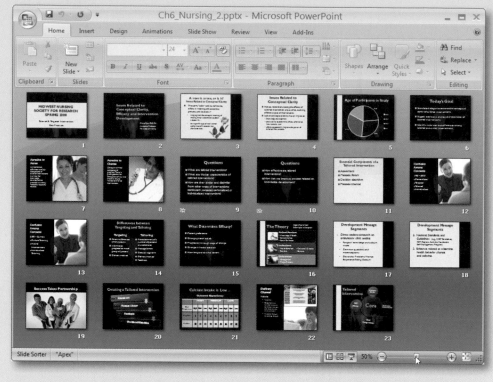

IF WE HAD TO PICK the top software packages that are globally recognized in every corporation, association, and educational institution, PowerPoint would head the list. PowerPoint has become synonymous with presentations and when used to its full potential, it is a powerful and effective tool for delivering information, yet most people have never been properly trained to use its rich features.

Usually it's a trial-by-fire situation—you have a presentation due at the end of the week, and either you modify a presentation that has already been delivered or you plod your way through an overused sample template provided with the software, haphazardly adding bullet points and titles. Maybe co-workers can point you in the right direction, or maybe they are in the same predicament that you're in. It's also possible that you've worked

with PowerPoint for 10 years, have a fairly adequate groove, and have never deviated. If a presentation is built based on any of these scenarios, chances are it's not the best that it could be.

We've written this book to help propel your presentations to new heights with all the new features available in Power-Point 2007. This completely reworked release has taken graphic design and the ability to customize just about everything to new levels. Haven't switched yet? Don't worry, most of the principles here will also apply to prior releases of PowerPoint, but you will need the current software to access projects on the CD-ROM.

We've noticed that most presenters have a general knowledge of how to use PowerPoint, but are missing some of the principles and techniques that can

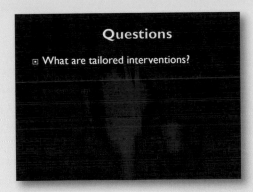

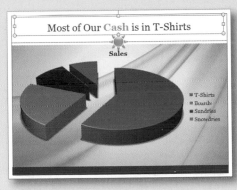

truly make their presentation educate, engage, and inspire. This book will give you the edge that you need to wow your audience. Our goal is to get right to the heart of making your slides look better and helping you communicate more effectively. Additionally, we realize that most presentations don't happen in the comfort of your workspace, so we've added steps to prep your presentations for multimedia delivery and travel.

Why Do I Need This Book?

You have a big presentation due and you want it to knock the socks off your audience. You have an idea of how to navigate in PowerPoint, but you need something better, and you need it now! We've written this book with you in mind. Often, we've found ourselves with less than adequate prep time and limited assets to prepare for high-profile presentations. We've taken these experiences (good and bad) and applied the latest release of PowerPoint to them to show you how you can get up and running as quickly as possible.

You'll be able to understand our theories and principles at a glance and follow our step-by-step tutorials in minutes, not hours. We've incorporated all of our project files on the enclosed CD-ROM,

as well as other, extra goodies so that you can work with the same files that you'll see in the full-color pages of *How to Wow with PowerPoint*.

How to Use This Book

Let's be honest: chances are that you're already in the middle of developing a presentation and you have a specific problem that you would like to solve. Go ahead and skip over to that chapter and find the help you need. However, to really get the most out of this book it's best to go through the chapters in order and experiment with all of the concepts and techniques that are available. Make sure to copy each chapter-specific project folder to your computer from the enclosed CD-ROM so that you'll navigate through the book with us and save your progress.

We've referred mostly to menu commands throughout the book, but always keep in mind that there are shortcut keys to accomplish many of the menu-command tasks. You'll also discover that you can accomplish things faster by right-clicking your mouse rather than always moving your cursor to and from the Ribbon. As you work through the pages of this book, experiment with different ways to access the commands that

you want to activate and decide what is most comfortable for you.

Our Goal

We hope that you will read through this book and follow along with the lessons and topics that we cover. After you've improved your PowerPoint skills, keep the book close at hand as a reference tool for a specific technique or principle to help polish your presentations. With a thorough knowledge of what works for you and your organization, you'll see a dramatic improvement in how quickly and easily you can create and modify your presentations and also in how they are received by your audience.

We didn't write this book for technical wizards or PowerPoint gurus, but for our friends, colleagues, and peers. We know that most of you have already created a PowerPoint presentation but want more for your efforts. Here we've attempted to package sound design practices and real-world experience into a friendly format that's easy to use. It would be great for everyone to have a graphic design department at their disposal for each presentation, and with this book you'll have everything you need to make it look like you did. ▨

1

TYPOGRAPHY, LAYOUT & DESIGN

It All Starts with Words on a Page

EVERY DAY WE'RE surrounded by good typography and design. Many times we're not conscious of things that are designed well, but we find ourselves drawn to them. Imagine if a caution sign at a factory were set in a red script typeface using all capital letters on a cobalt blue background. Even if

the sign were prominently displayed, no one would be able to or have any desire to read it. We recently worked with a law enforcement agency to update its brand and overall graphic identity. When we discussed the navy blue jackets that would display bold yellow letters that spelled out POLICE, there was no room for getting fancy. These uniforms were designed well, with their audience in mind. They had high-contrast, easy-to-read colors. The typeface chosen was bold and set very large. Words were chosen very carefully, and the overall design was kept extremely simple. Why? In a split second people seeing the jackets might have to determine how to react in a potentially life-

threatening situation. Good typography, layout, and design are not only good for business and educational purposes, but can save lives.

What's in a Theme?

Themes can contain a color palette, font selections, effects, images, and more. Themes are a great place to start when it comes to building a presentation quickly. Themes can be modified to act as the foundation for a custom presentation that is more appropriate for your audience.

When is the Font Comic Sans Appropriate?

The answer is simple—*never*. Some fonts just scream cheesy, amateur production, and this is one of them. Choosing the right fonts can be half the battle in the quest for strong design. Going beyond the default set and installing new fonts can also make a bold statement.

Comic Sans

Clarity is Key

Organizing your information in a way that makes your message clear is paramount. Even if you are the most charismatic speaker around, you can still leave your audience confused and turned off by a poorly organized presentation. The clearer your slides are, the easier it will be for you to take a quick glance at them if you lose your train of thought and leave no one in the audience the wiser. The principles of organizational clarity can be reinforced with technical clarity settings as well as visual clarity principles.

It Looks Cool, but I Can't Read It.

We've seen many really cool typography books that highlight designs that cram type together to make textures. We've also seen slides that have magnificent backgrounds, but we could barely see the type, much less comfortably read it. Readability is key. If your audience is engaged in deciphering the hieroglyphics that you've presented, they're not paying attention to what you've just said.

Slide Layout—5 Do's & 5 Don'ts

When used properly, every tool can achieve the desired result. When used improperly, a tool can create a very undesirable effect. A hammer is a great tool for installing a new roof on your house. That same hammer might have an undesirable effect if your dentist used it to install your next filling. Don't hammer your audience with bad slides.

Do—Keep it Simple

Simple slides will help guide your audience to your desired outcome. Think of the slides like road signs on an unfamiliar highway. Their message should be brief. Your audience is running at 75 miles per hour; their minds should not be cluttered up with several images competing for attention. Next time you are on a highway, peek at the billboards. Which ones are the most effective?

Do—Stay Consistent

Consistency will allow your audience to focus on your content and not what font you decide to use next or where in the rainbow your next background color will fall. Font colors, sizes, weights, and styles should remain consistent throughout your presentation. A color palette should be decided upon and adhered to. Remember our road sign analogy. What if every road sign you passed in an unfamiliar city had a different font, color, and layout. How quickly would you be able to identify where your next turn should be? To see at a glance how consistent your presentation is, view it in Slide Sorter view.

Do—Build Your Presentation for Your Audience

If you are planning on building a presentation that is meant to stand alone without a presenter, your text and imagery must be able to act as a self-guided tour. Remember, PowerPoint is a tool that works best when kept simple and brief. If you want to pass along a detailed report for your audience, then use a page layout program and create handouts. If you plan on being there to present the information, think of yourself as the anchor on the evening news. You are delivering the story, and the slides are behind you to help reinforce your key points.

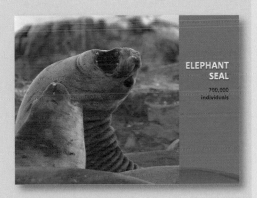

Do—Keep Bullet Points Short and Clear

Most people will zone out or get distracted during a presentation. Make sure that if they do, they can glance at your bullet points and understand where you are going. In just a few words you should attempt to make a clear, complete thought. Random buzzwords are great for conference room chatter; however, they will not make your audience understand the point you are trying to make.

Do—Use Beautiful High Quality Images

Junky, poorly lit, out-of-focus, discolored, low-resolution images say one thing to your audience: you're not worth my fine china. Here is a paper plate. Enjoy. Large, beautiful, and powerful images are the ones that command attention. Think of a gallery exhibition of fine photography. How would you react if you walked along a long white wall of perfectly mounted photographs and halfway through you saw a photocopy of an image that once appeared in a newspaper tacked up?

Don't—Use Too Many Elements on a Slide

Break down complex ideas to their simplest forms. Charts with gobs of icons and arrows pointing in all different directions will confuse your audience. Paragraphs of text will tempt people to read a slide while you are trying to engage them. If it is absolutely necessary to have a large amount of content, break it up among several slides, keeping each slide clean and simple so it's easy to follow.

Don't—Build a Presentation Based on Bullets

Presentations that consist of slide after slide, each with a series of bullets, will bore your audience into complacency. Use bullet slides sparingly, broken up with large beautiful images—or wake up your audience with a slide that contains nothing but a clear concise statement, in HUGE type.

Don't—Place Images Randomly

There are many ways to lay out a presentation. We've seen highly effective presentations that use words very sparingly and center all text and images on a simple white background. We've also seen well-laid-out presentations where images are placed based on a grid system. Either way the audience comes to expect images to be in a certain area. This expectation allows them to focus on your content and message more clearly.

Don't—Use Slides Presented on Screen as a Handout

If you prepare your slides so they will also function as a handout, then you probably have too much information on them. If you need to cover important points, you can either build your presentation with detailed speaking notes for each slide (or series of slides) or create a similarly branded handout in a page layout program to be distributed at the closing of your presentation.

Don't—Overdo Word Art

Try to keep type as clean and readable as possible. There are tons of possibilities for making type look cool and funky. Make sure that when you step back from your screen, the type that you just jazzed up doesn't get lost in the background or get so jumbled up with depth and shadows that it's difficult to read.

Using PowerPoint Themes

Using PowerPoint Themes can give you a jumpstart on a great presentation. You can modify an existing theme to differentiate your presentation from any others or create a new custom presentation. The good news is there is a wealth of resources to help you find all the elements you'll need.

What Makes a Good Theme?

The two things that you should look for in a theme are simplicity and versatility. The simpler your theme, the less distracting it will be from your content and message. Also, look for theme colors that are harmonious with each other. The great thing about PowerPoint Themes is that if you love the look of a theme but the color of the fonts and accents are not exactly what you want, you can change them.

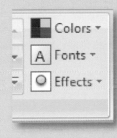

How to Start

Do you have existing corporate colors? Do you have a team logo or school mascot that you would like your presentation to complement? Is your presentation to physicians or engineers—sports enthusiasts or recording artists? Is your audience very familiar with your Web site? These are some of the questions to ask yourself before you set out on a theme quest. Existing branding can determine which colors and designs you choose. Knowing your audience can also help you determine what colors and designs are appropriate.

Where to Look

Start right within PowerPoint. Once you have your basic slide outline put together, make sure that you are in the Normal Slide view and click the Design Tab in your Ribbon. You'll see several thumbnails in the Theme group. Roll over some of the thumbnails with your mouse and watch your slides integrate into each theme before your eyes. Make sure to allow your computer's processor to catch up to your rollovers. If you see a layout that fits your audience and message, click it.

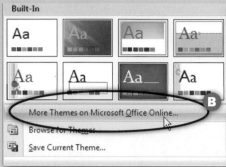

Taking the Search Online

In the Theme group, click the more arrow in the scroll bar next to the theme thumbnails **A**. You can search on Microsoft's online library by selecting the More Themes on Microsoft Office Online button **B**. This will open up your browser and allow you to search for themes (or templates that you can save as themes) by keyword and category.

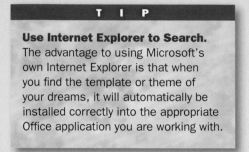

> **TIP**
>
> **Use Internet Explorer to Search.**
> The advantage to using Microsoft's own Internet Explorer is that when you find the template or theme of your dreams, it will automatically be installed correctly into the appropriate Office application you are working with.

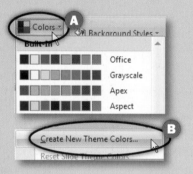

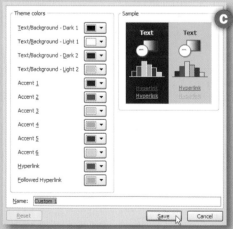

Modifying to Match Your Style

Under the Design tab in the Ribbon, click the Colors drop-down menu under the Themes Group **A**. Roll over some of the color swatch groups and monitor how these colors change the look of your slide theme. Select a color palette that is close to your desired colors. If the colors are close but not exactly what you want, then click the Create New Theme Colors button under the Colors drop-down menu **B**. This will open up a window that will allow you to modify the colors to your liking, and give you visual feedback in the sample area on the right **C**. ▦

Selecting and Installing Fonts

When building a presentation, chances are you randomly select a font. You'll pick one from the list, and then eventually try another. If you truly understand the characteristics of fonts, then you can make better decisions about which font to use. Picking the "right" font is a combination of several factors. You'll need to weigh issues such as readability with others like aesthetics and style. Additionally, you'll have to keep in mind the availability of the fonts and whether they support all of the characters you need in your presentation.

Serif

Sans Serif

Serif Versus Sans Serif

With fonts there are two major distinctions: serif and sans serif. Serif fonts (such as Times, Garamond, and New York) are generally easier for your audience to read. They have small strokes at the end of the larger strokes. The alternative is sans-serif fonts (such as Gill Sans, Helvetica, and Arial). They have a cleaner style and generally use even-weighted lines.

Serif

- Are easier to read in print;
- Offer more fonts to pick from;
- Are modeled after handwritten texts and printing-press type;
- Are often favored by traditionalists.

Sans Serif

- Present possible character–thickness problems;
- Have been optimized for use on-screen;
- Can usually compress more text into smaller space;
- Read better at small sizes.

ascender · Juxtapose · baseline · x-height · descender

X-Height

One of the most defining characteristics of a font is its x-height (the distance from the top of a lowercase x to the bottom). The x is a clean letter, which is easy to discern, and it does a lot to describe the character of a font. The visual distinctiveness of a font is judged by its x-height and also the height of its ascenders (the letters l and t) and descenders (y and p), both which grow from the center of the space occupied by the letter.

INSIGHT

Learn More about Type. Want to learn more about type? Check out Microsoft's typography area on its Web site at www.microsoft.com/typography.

regular **bold**
italic ***bold italic***
condensed light

Font Weight

A truly useful font will have multiple weights. A font generally has a book (or Roman) weight. A font family may also contain Light, Medium, Bold, Black, Italic, and more alternates. These alternate weights are useful as they provide more design options without mixing fonts.

Gill Sans   Georgia

Myriad   **Impact**

HelveticaNeue   **Verdana**

Trebuchet   **Futura**

On-Screen Appearance

First and foremost, you are designing your presentation to be viewed on-screen. You'll want to test out fonts to see how they look on your computer display. If the fonts are too busy or have too many elaborate serifs, you may want to make them inactive or remove them from your computer. Most modern fonts look very good on-screen; these include Gill Sans, Georgia, Myriad, Impact, Helvetica Neue, Verdana, Trebuchet, and Futura.

Style

Ask yourself, what is the presentation all about? Draw up a list of 10–20 adjectives that describe your presentation or subject matter. Use these words to help select fonts. You can use a more distinctive display font for the title pages, but you should select a cleaner body font for the bullets and secondary text.

Finding Fonts Online

There are lots of font Web sites out there to choose from. Here are a few places to get fonts for use in your presentation. These are where we personally shop for new fonts.

- www.chank.com (free and for sale)
- www.fonthead.com (free and for sale)
- www.myfonts.com (for sale)
- www.t26.com (for sale)
- www.adobe.com/type/index.html (for sale)
- www.girlswhowearglasses.com (free)

Installing Your Selected Font

Once you find a font that you want to install, you'll need activate the font. If you are using a font manager, skip ahead to the next section. Otherwise, you can activate a font using the following steps. Make sure that the fonts you need are copied to your local computer.

1. From the Start menu, choose Control Panel, then select the Appearance and Themes category.

2. In the See Also panel (in the upper left corner), choose Fonts.

3. From the File menu, select Install New Font.

4. In the navigation box, select the drive, then folder that contains the fonts you want to load. Select the fonts you want and click OK.

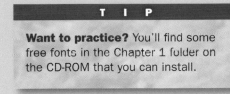

TIP

Want to practice? You'll find some free fonts in the Chapter 1 folder on the CD-ROM that you can install.

How Many Fonts to Load

When we look at most peoples' computers, we are amazed at how many fonts they have active on their systems. While most of our computers have 3,000 or more fonts loaded on the hard drive, we rarely keep more than 75 active at any time. If you have hundreds (or even thousands) of fonts loaded, you'll have an unmanageable mess. A better idea is to keep your fonts organized with a font manager.

Be sure to check out one of these tools:

- Extensis Suitcase for Windows—www.extensis.com
- MainType—www.high-logic.com
- Font Wrangler—www.mindworkshop.com

Replacing Fonts Globally and Locally

Making Font Changes Is Simple When Your Entire Presentation Is Built on a Theme

1. Prepare Your Files

In order to complete this exercise (and others in this chapter) you'll need to copy the files to your local computer. From the project CD-ROM, open the HTW Project Files folder and copy the Chapter 1 folder to your local hard drive. This folder contains all of the files needed for this chapter. Open the file Ch1_Welcome_to_Antarctica.pptx and switch to slide 4.

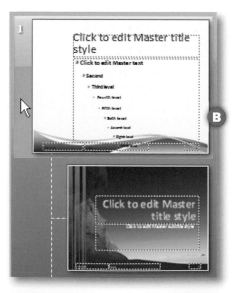

2. Master Your Fonts

Under the View Tab in the Ribbon, click the Slide Master button in the Presentation Views group **A**. Then click the first slide in the thumbnail view on the left-hand side of your window **B**.

3. Select Font to Modify

In the main presentation window, select the title or bullet point that you would like to modify. Hover your cursor over the selected text and slowly roll above it. A small editing toolbar will appear that will allow you to modify the selected text's font.

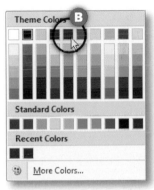

4. Modify Text

Within the mini-toolbar you can modify the font, color, size, level of indentation, and more. Make the font bold by clicking the **B** button **A**. This modification will make a global change on all of the slides using the bullet level that you modified. Also, you can change the font to a dark blue color in the theme **B**.

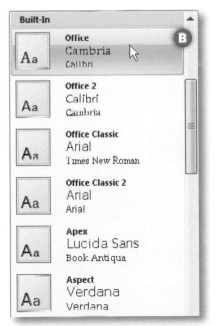

INSIGHT

Undesired Ragging. When you globally change your fonts, your lines of text may break in unexpected ways due to subtle differences in font properties so check them carefully.

5. Global Quick Change

Go to the View tab in the Ribbon and then select the Normal button in the Presentation Views group **A**. Once normal mode has been selected, click the Design tab in the Ribbon. Click the Fonts drop-down menu in the Themes group. Roll over each group to see a live preview in your main slide view **B**. Select the theme called Office. Click each slide thumbnail to see how this global font theme has affected the overall look of your presentation.

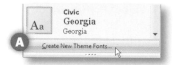

6. Create New Theme Fonts

If your organization has a style guide that specifies a headline font and a body copy font for presentations, you can create your own theme fonts. With the fonts drop-down menu open in the Themes group, select the Create New Theme Fonts button **A**. A new window will open that will allow you to select a main Heading font as well as a main Body font. Select a font from each drop-down menu. In the Name field rename your font theme MyFontTheme and select save **B**. Next, click the Fonts drop-down menu in the Themes group. Your new font theme is available for all future presentations **C**.

7. Local Font Change

Click the slide 3 thumbnail in your presentation. Click the text on the bottom of the slide. Next, click in front of the first letter and drag to the right to select all of the letters in the text box. With the text selected, click the Format tab beneath the Drawing Tools tab in the Ribbon. Click the Text Effects button in the Word Art Group. Select one of the Reflection presets from the drop-down menu **A**. ▦

Organizing Information for Clarity

The main goal for just about every presentation is to supply information to an audience in a way that is easily understood. The other goal is to motivate an audience to take some sort of action. To achieve both of these goals, you must constantly take a step back and ask yourself, "Am I presenting this information in its clearest and simplest form?"

What and Where Is the Grid?

Print designers are trained to build layouts based on a grid. You can use these same principles when laying out your PowerPoint slides. Under the View tab in the Ribbon in the Show/Hide group are two check boxes called Ruler and Gridlines. When both boxes are checked, you'll be able to see a series of lines that will help you position elements accurately on your slides and slide masters.

Modifying the Grid and Guides

Right-click anywhere in your main slide viewing window and a menu will appear. Click the Grid and Guides button. This will open up a dialog box that will allow you to modify the grid and drawing guides that you can create to help layout your slides.

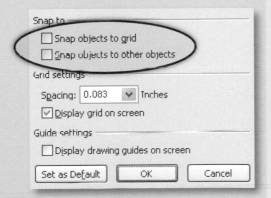

Snapping and Grid Settings

In the Snap to group, the Snap objects to grid and Snap objects to other objects check boxes will cause items to align precisely to the grid lines that appear on your slide, or to other objects that are adjacent to the object you are moving. The Grid settings drop-down menu will allow you to select from default grid spacing or type in your own custom spacing parameters. Display grid on screen will allow you to position items precisely during the creation of your presentation, but will not be visible in presentation mode.

Drawing Guides

You'll notice that in addition to the grid you can see two lines that intersect at the center of your slide. Those are your drawing guides. You can modify these by clicking and dragging them. To add additional drawing guides, Control click on an existing guide and drag it to your desired position. In the sample presentation we have added two additional guides to help with layout.

The Rule of Thirds

Directors, designers, and photographers compose their work based on a simple grid that is split into thirds at all times. In fact, many cameras have this same grid build right into their viewfinder to aid in composition. When composing a slide or selecting photography for a slide, it is usually pleasing to the eye to have a dominant feature of the photo, illustration or text fall on or near a gridline.

Drawing a Grid of Thirds

You can quickly divide your layout into thirds by moving the Drawing Guides that we discussed earlier. Make sure that your drawing guides are visible by right-clicking in your main slide window and selecting the Display drawing guides on-screen checkbox in your Grid and Guides window. Then drag the vertical guide to the left to about the 1.66" mark. Don't worry if it is not exactly at that point. Create a new line by Control dragging the vertical line to the right to the 1.66" point on the right side of the slide. Repeat this process to create two horizontal lines that are on the 1.25" point on the top and bottom of your slide.

Using the Grid of Thirds

The grid is there for you as a guide. You'll run into situations where you'll need to deviate from the grid in order to accommodate certain slide elements. However, when you are trying to decide where to place an image or text, the grid will lead you in the right direction. Keep in mind that you don't always have to have the edge of a photo on a gridline. If you are using a large photo or a full-screen photo, use the grid to position the most dominant element or the image itself.

Using the Grid of Thirds for Text Placement

Use the gridlines to help you decide where to position text or to align a series of bullets on a page **A**. You can also use this grid to place short blocks of text on a full-screen photo **B**. The Rule of Thirds is not absolute, but in most cases it can really help a design.

Using Color and Shape to Define Key Points

Within your theme, you'll have a color palette. You can use this color palette to decide which colors to use to help define key points. In this example there were originally three text bullet points to explain the summer temperature of three different research stations. By using SmartArt (located in the Illustrations Group under the Insert tab) you can illustrate bullet points in a clearer, more visual manner. We'll talk more about SmartArt in Chapter 2.

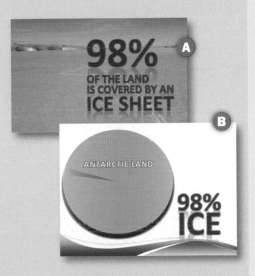

Adding Impact to Statistical Information

Statistical information tends to be dry and forgettable. Using a high-impact photo or illustration that supports your statistic will make the numbers and statements more meaningful and memorable **A**. Many times it will be difficult to find the perfect photo to support your statistic. In cases like this a simple chart with type set very large can have a great impact on your audience **B**. ▦

Improving Readability

Living and working in the Washington, D.C., area has allowed us to enjoy countless presentations that include the colors red, white, and blue. Those colors can work if used correctly, or they can embody a cardinal sin in readability. Color is just one parameter that can affect readability. Text size, contrast, texture, kerning, and leading can also affect your audience's ability to read your content.

Good Colors Gone Bad

While we're quite fond of red, white, and blue, these colors will "vibrate" when placed on top of one another. High color contrast is important when deciding on text and background colors. Your goal is to achieve instant recognition of your message. If the colors of your text and background are competing with each other for attention, it will make the text difficult to read. Also notice how a serif typeface set too small is difficult to read.

Image-Based Backgrounds

It has become quite trendy to use a photograph as a background for slides. The key to pulling this off is to remember that there needs to be a high level of contrast between your image or texture and your text. Select a photograph that already has an area that is soft in texture and includes only subtle changes in color. Overlay a semitransparent shape (Insert tab) on your background image. You can adjust the color and transparency by selecting the shape, right-clicking, and then selecting the Format Shape button. Now you can place text on top of your shape. This will provide the contrast that you need to separate your text from the background image.

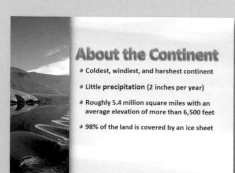

Texture-Based Backgrounds

If you intend to use a texture of any kind for a slide or shape background, make sure that the color or contrast does not compete with the text or images on your page. If the texture does not add anything to your overall theme or message, consider dropping it or swapping it out for a solid color. Avoid using a logo that's repeated to form a pattern. It's incredibly distracting and cheapens your logo.

Spreading Out your Content

When it's important to have a large amount of text in a presentation, it's better to spread the text over several slides then to try to cram it all onto one **A**. Divide your text at the most natural breaking point to prevent the front row from reading ahead and the back row from squinting to see the small font size **B**.

Adjusting Paragraph Spacing

To prevent all of your text or bullets from running together on the page, separate each line and each paragraph individually. You can make these adjustments in your Slide Master view by selecting the first thumbnail on the left side of your view panel and right-clicking in the text box with your bullet hierarchy. Select the Paragraph button and adjust the line spacing so that the space between paragraphs is visually greater than the space between lines.

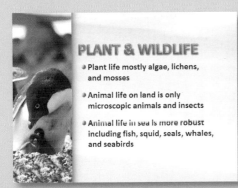

Alignment

Hands down, the easiest text to read is text aligned to the left. When you have to incorporate several lines, it's best to stay in the fast lane by aligning your blocks of text to the left and staying consistent with this approach throughout the presentation. However, when using less text and larger typefaces (which is what we hope you'll be doing anyway), alignment is less of an issue. It's easy to decipher small bites of texts regardless of what alignment they are formatted in.

Character Spacing

Sometimes after modifying a font with word art or using faux bold on a font (using the **B** button in the type toolbar) you'll notice that the letters look a little too close together. You can modify the character spacing (also known as tracking). Select the type, then choose the Home tab from the Ribbon. Click Character Spacing to choose a new value; positive numbers increase spacing, negative numbers decrease it. This option will also come in handy to expand or contract the letter spacing when you have an unusually ornate or decorative font.

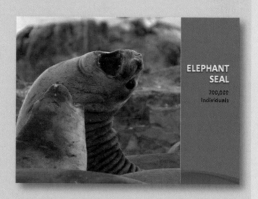

Creating a Hierarchy of Importance

Take a step back and look at your slide. Do the type and graphical elements compete with one another? It's important to guide your audience visually through your layout by attributing a hierarchy of importance using size, color, and contrast. The eye has a tendency to land on a full-opacity, large image first. Then it goes to the highest contrast, largest typeface, and so on. If a high-contrast headline, phrase, or number is set very large and surrounded by negative space, the eye will have a tendency to begin scanning the page there (even if a large photo or illustration accompanies it).

Grouping and Aligning

Avoid at all costs placing items randomly on a slide **A**. If you have a series of photos (even if they're different sizes), find a way to align them. You can select all the photos and then within the Arrange group under the Format tab, select the Align button. You can then align the photos consistently with each other as well as distribute them evenly vertically or horizontally **B**. Refer back to your rule of thirds to help you with placement. ▥

Adding and Customizing Shadows

Customizing Shadows Can Improve Readability

1. Determine the Need for Shadows

Many objects will benefit from the addition of a drop-shadow. Oftentimes on a slide, you will have text or an object that is placed over a textured background (such as a photo). Because colors in the background may be similar to the color of the overlaying object, readability can become an issue. This is referred to as "type on pattern." If you have text or logos that do not significantly contrast with the background, the addition of a shadow will help.

2. Select the Logo

Switch to slide 24 in the presentation and examine the logo. Notice how the blues of the logo are similar to the background? A shadow will help the logo stand out a bit more. Click the ASF logo so it is active.

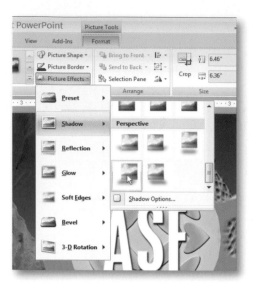

3. Add the Shadow

In order to add a shadow, click the Format tab in the Ribbon. Next click Picture Effects in the Picture Style group. Choose "Shadow," then scroll down to the Perspective group. Select Perspective Diagonal Lower Left to apply a shadow preset. A drop-shadow is added, and the logo now looks like it is casting a shadow on the snow. The effect is good, but can be refined.

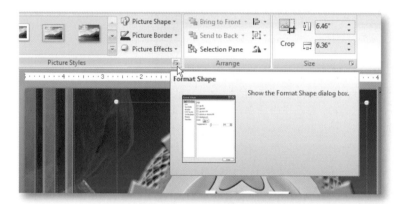

4. Access the Format Shape Dialog Box

The drop-shadow can be further customized by accessing the Format Shape dialog box. The dialog box is somewhat hidden, but offers powerful controls in one window. To access it, click the small box and arrow at the bottom of the Picture Styles group. A new window opens.

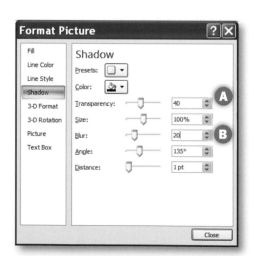

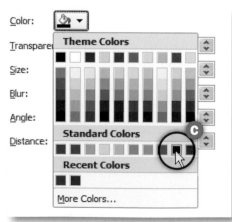

5. Customize the Shadow

In the Format Shape dialog box, click the shadow tab. You can now customize the shadow. Darken the shadow by reducing Transparency to 40 percent **A**. Soften the shadow by increasing the Blur to 20 pt **B**. Finally, you should customize the shadow color. Shadows are rarely pure black; rather, they pick up color from the surrounding areas. Click the paint bucket icon and choose Dark Blue from the Standard Colors list **C**. ▣

Using Bullet Points Effectively

While bullet points are the staple ingredient of many presentations, they must be used properly. Too many bullet points can bore and confuse your audience (we refer to bullet points as open captions for the thinking impaired). It is important to know when (and when not) to use bullets as well as how to properly balance the use of text on screen. Here are our rules for using bullet points effectively.

When to Use Bullets

A bullet point is a phrase meant to help your audience remember the key points of your presentation. Bullet points should be used as triggers or memory joggers, not as a replacement for your speech. Many presenters feel a need to put too many words on the screen. In fact, they overload their bullet points until they have a line of text for almost every point they make. This approach is often referred to as "death by bullets," and is one of audiences' major complaints about presenters. For nearly every presenter, the use of shorter (and fewer) bullet points will benefit their presentation style.

PLANT & WILDLIFE

- Plant life mostly algae, lichens, and mosses
- On land are only microscopic animals and insects
- Sea is more robust including fish, squid, seals, whales, and seabirds

What Makes a Good Bullet

Remember, your bullets should be kept short. This means you'll likely use one to seven words for each bullet. A bullet doesn't need to be a full sentence, but it should not be a jumbled mess of abbreviations and abrupt phrases. The easiest way to generate a good bullet point is to think like an audience member. Ask yourself, what phrase would you write down after hearing that part of the presentation?

How Many Bullets to Use

It is important to not clutter your slide with too many bullet points. If your slide does include bullets, we recommend using between three and seven bullets per page. There is no law that says you must fit all bullet points on one page. It is more than acceptable to equally divide your bullet points for a topic and spread them across multiple slides. In this case, just keep a consistent title at the top of each slide in the set to help your audience's comprehension.

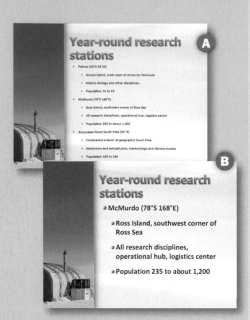

Design for Readability

It is important to keep your bullets large enough to read. The font size should be smaller than the title on the page (smaller text size denotes order of importance—this is information that supports the title or topic). However, you must keep the bullets large enough to read **A**. Our advice is to design for the back of the room **B**. The most important decision-makers usually arrive later (because they are busy), and they sit toward the back of a presentation. Make sure your text is big enough to be easily seen by them.

> ### TIP
>
> **Test Your Bullets.** If you'd like to "try out" a presentation, you can launch your slide show (F5), then step away from your computer. In fact, you'll want to stand at least 20 feet away and look at the screen. Can you still read your presentation?

Be Consistent

Many presenters deviate from their presentation's style when creating bullet points. It is important that you establish rules for bullets, so you (or team members) do not drift. Here are common problems to avoid:

- *Inconsistent capitalization*—Are you using sentence case (where only the first word and proper nouns receive capital letters) or Title Case (where most words are capitalized)?
- *Inconsistent punctuation*—Are you using periods at the end of each bullet? **A**
- *Improper use of formatting*—Are you using **bold** and *italics* in your bullets? If so, be sure you use them for the same reasons in all cases **B**.
- *Failure to proofread*—As most users rush through creating their bullet points, they tend to make spelling errors. Be sure to proofread to catch both grammar and spelling errors (don't be overly reliant on the built-in spell checker) **C**.

When Not to Use Bullets

There are plenty of reasons to not use bullet points on a slide. It is a good idea to challenge yourself regularly to decide if you really need them. For example, is a powerful photo enough? Would a chart better illustrate the data? Can a product sample or demo be used? Would a handout or brochure deliver your message better? There is nothing wrong with bullet points, but it is important to remember that they are only one part of an effective presentation. 🁢

Customizing Bullets

PowerPoint Offers Several Bullets to Choose From

1. Select the Bullets to Modify

You need to select a slide with bullets that need modifying. Select slide 4, which contains a block of text with bullets. Click in the text block to activate it, then press Ctrl+A to select all of the text.

2. Customize the Bullets

Click the Home tab to access text controls. From the Paragraph Group click the arrow next to the Bullets button to choose a different bullet style. You can select from the available list or choose Bullets and Numbering for more options.

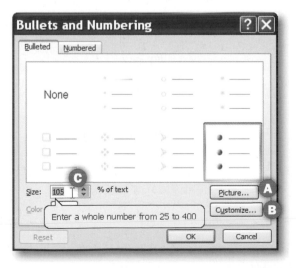

3. Select an Option

You can modify several properties from the dialog box including size and color. Click Picture **A** to browse available image bullets (checking the box Include content from Office Online gives even more options). You can also click Customize **B** to pick a different character or symbol from the font. For this presentation, change the bullets to 105 percent **C** to make them slightly larger, then click OK. 🁢

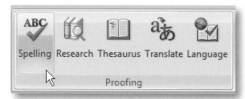

Spell Check and Special Characters

Text Will Often Need Special Tweaks to Achieve Perfection

1. Check Spelling for Your Slide Show

PowerPoint has a built-in spell check that you can run to look for spelling errors. In the Ribbon, click the Review tab. From the Proofing group, click the Spelling button. The Spelling window opens and PowerPoint highlights the first misspelling in the presentation.

2. Fix Errors

We purposely left two spelling errors to illustrate how to correct them. In the Spelling window, the first misspelling is selected. In the context of the sentence, Reech should be Reach. You can select the proper replacement from the Change to: list. Click "Change" to substitute the word and move onto the next. The second misspelling is Tempurature; select the correct replacement from the Change to list and click Change.

INSIGHT

Ewe Mite Style Have Eros. Just because the check spelling command says your slides are error free, don't become overconfident. Computers are not very good at catching grammar and logic errors. Always read through your slides to look for errors (better yet get a colleague to double-check them).

3. Access Special Characters

Sometimes you'll need special characters to communicate meaning. While many letters and popular symbols are on your keyboard, many other are not (such as ¢, ©, ™, º, £, etc.). Fortunately, most characters are accessible through a keyboard map. On slide 17, there is a missing degrees symbol (°). In the Palmer Station text block, click between the 55 and the F. Then select the Insert tab in the Ribbon. From the Text group click Symbol **A**. Choose the ° symbol **B** and click Insert, then click Close to add the missing character. ⌨

CAUTION

Missing Characters. If specific characters come up missing, be sure to check your settings. In the Spelling box, be sure to check the Subset drop-down menu to see different character options.

2

TABLES, CHARTS & GRAPHS

Presenting Information with Visual Clarity

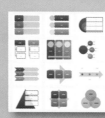

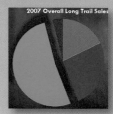
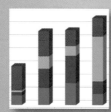
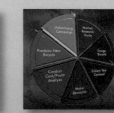

CHARTS AND GRAPHS—these words alone can put an audience to sleep. Most PowerPoint users clutter up the screen so badly that their audience can't help but "zone out" during the presentation. A cluttered screen can confuse and even annoy your audience. Informational graphics need to be clear and concise. In this chapter, we'll show you some common mistakes and provide examples of how specific kinds of graphics can inform (and impress) your audience with clear data and attractive design.

Keep It Simple

Simple is better. Avoid using too many effects on your type and chart segments. A nice clean design is easier to understand and presents you and your information in the best possible way. Think about how impressive a business suit looks with a well-chosen tie or scarf. Select your accent of color in the same manner. Then carry the whole design aesthetic into a chart. The secret to great charts is to keep them well dressed and elegant.

Keep It Focused

Just what are you trying to say? A good informational graphic like a pie chart or bar graph focuses on a single topic. The goal here is to make your graphics as clear as possible. This means filling the slide with a large graphic to impart your data. Keep the number of data points limited and try to simplify your focus (to, say, a decade of historical data instead of a century). Large-overview graphics are important, but so are the close-ups.

More Is Better

We don't mean more on the slide; rather, we recommend using more slides when necessary. We once worked with a large telephone company that wanted to explain it's entire organizational chart on a single slide. Sure, a simplistic overview would have worked, but that's not what they did. Rather, the executive

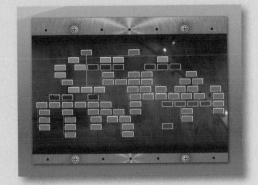

talked for 30 minutes to one organizational chart that had approximately 400 boxes (complete with 6 point type and connecting lines). The only reason the audience didn't stand up and walk out was that doing so would have meant getting fired. Remember it takes far more work to cram 10 slides of material onto one slide than it does to build 10 simple slides that are visually clear. If you want to make information easier for your audience to follow, keep your slides to a single chart or graph as opposed to ganging multiple items onto one slide.

Double-Check It

Data errors in your information graphics can be deadly. You can find yourself having to honor a price you never intended to offer—shareholders could expect bigger returns—or you might just end up looking like you flunked the fifth grade. It is critical to review your math and formulas. Don't be afraid to pull out that old solar calculator and put it to work crunching the numbers (after all percentages don't usually add up to more than 100). A good presenter uses the computer as an assistant, but maintains healthy skepticism and double-checks his or her own work.

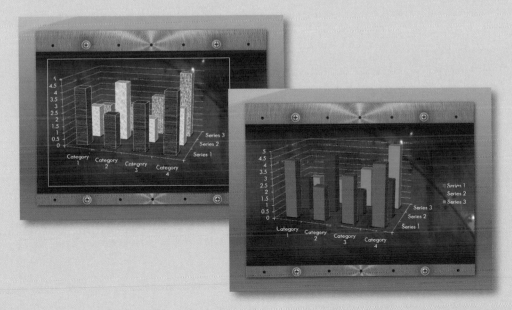

Choosing the Right Graphic Format

If your audience is wading through text-based statistical information on the screen then they're not paying attention to what you are saying. Instead, convert your data into a visual. The most important factor in determining which data graphic you choose is clarity. Choosing the right one can help your audience decipher your data and direct them to a specific point that you are trying to make.

Guide Your Audience

We've seen slide or chart titles that simply say something to the effect of "sales trends" above a bar or line chart. The chart may visibly display an upward or downward trend, but what do you want the audience to focus on? Titling your slide something like "Sales Spike with School Start" gives it a one-two punch that will guide them. Growth may already be obvious in your chart, but your audience can make a more complex determination based on your title and your data combined.

Keep It Simple with a Clustered Column

If you want to compare amounts of data (perhaps the number of bikes sold online versus at retail stores), a vertical column chart can do this very clearly. It's also possible to demonstrate multiple comparisons clearly with a bar chart that uses color and labeling to differentiate. For example, you can quickly demonstrate the sales performance of three different bikes sold online versus at retail stores using a clustered column chart. Although 3-D charts look slick, be careful. Many times a fancy 3-D chart can make instant comprehension of data more difficult.

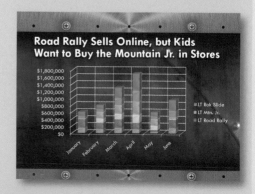

Use Stacked Columns for Multiple Items

Stacked column charts can demonstrate how multiple items arrive at a total when combined. For example, we could see the total sales of three bikes over the course of six months and at the same time see which bike was the better seller during any particular month.

Use Line Charts for Time

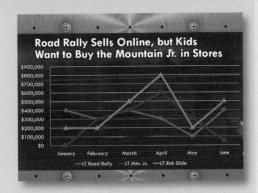

When there are multiple changes that need to be illustrated over time, a line chart often works best. The audience can follow the progression of change and very easily pinpoint where the change occurred. You can also visually compare multiple components using color or line thickness to differentiate data. Again, be careful with the ability to move into the 3-D realm here. Line charts can become very confusing when they are viewed at an angle.

Combine Chart Types

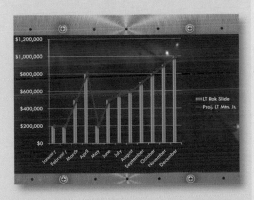

You can build a visual story by combining two different messages in the same chart. For example, you can use a clustered column chart to show actual sales over the course of a year for each bicycle. You can then overlay a line chart to show what the projected sales for each bicycle were. This combination can help lead the audience to some conclusions about the success of a product over time based on what was initially expected.

Clarify Duration with Bar Charts

If you want to show the wear on a bicycle tire or anything else over time, turn your columns on their sides by selecting a bar chart. Your audience reads left to right and it's easier to comprehend things over time this way (think timeline). Multiple comparisons are also easy to decipher at a glance. For example, we could measure bicycle tire wear for a 110-mile race as well as heat buildup and vibration for several different tires to determine the best overall performance.

Creating Tables

Organizing Text for
Visual Clarity

TIP

Add It Up. If you need to add a row to the end of a table, you can click in the last cell of the last row. Press the tab key to create (and move to) a new row.

1. Add a Table

A table is a great way to organize a lot of text so it is easier to read through and comprehend. With a table, you use columns to organize words and numbers. These columns help to establish relationships between categories of numbers. Additionally, a table can offer a quick synopsis of the data. Adding a table to a slide is very easy as long as you know how many cells you will need. To determine this, do a quick pen-and-paper sketch of what you think will go into the table. While you can always modify the table in the future, it's a good idea to get started by making the design as close as possible to what you'll need for the end product. To get started, open the Ch2_Long_Trail.pptx presentation, and click on the slide 6 Thumbnail. Next, choose the Insert tab. In the Tables group, click the Table button and choose Insert Table. The Insert Table window opens and prompts you for input. Enter 3 into the Number of columns field and 10 into the Number of rows field. Click OK to add the table.

	FY '06	FY '07
Sales Revenue	$136.40	$165.30
Licensing Revenue	$34.20	$46.30
Dealer Fees	$24.40	$35.70
TOTAL REVENUE	$195.00	$247.30
Manufacturing	$87.40	$98.45
Marketing	$38.37	$56.35
TOTAL FEES	$125.77	$154.80
TOTAL	$69.23	$92.50

2. Enter Data

Text can be manually entered into a table or pasted from another document. To get practice with navigating through a table, you will enter text. In the table you have created, enter the information at left. You can type in a field, then press tab to shift to the next cell.

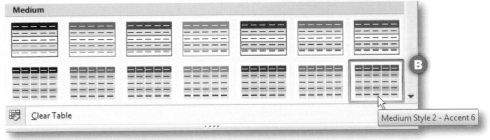

3. Use Styles

One way to quickly format a table is to use styles. A table style combines multiple styling options (such as colors and formatting) into a single click. PowerPoint provides you with a gallery of styles to browse and choose from. On slide 6, click on your newly created table so it is selected. The Table Tools Design tab is automatically selected. In the Table Styles group you have several choices (hover your mouse over the different styles to see them previewed). Click the More button **A** to preview the full list of styles. From the Medium group, choose Medium Style 2 – Accent 6 **B** and click once. The table is now formatted with the style; a few additional changes will further enhance its clarity.

4. Apply Additional Formatting

By formatting cells, we can further clarify the data layout. With the table still selected, select the Table Tools Design tab. Check the box next to First Column in the Table Styles option **A**; this darkens the first column, which helps distinguish it as labels. Then check the box next to Total Row, which bolds the last column and reverses the text over a solid color. These two changes help format the text information more clearly **B**.

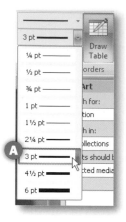

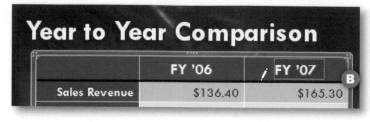

5. Format Borders

PowerPoint allows you to change the colors of borders. These changes can be useful to draw attention to specific cells and highlight information. First, let's offset the header row of the cell by underlining it. Click on the table to select it and then choose the Table Tools Design tab. In the Draw Borders group modify the following options: set the Pen color to black, change the Pen Style to a solid line; then set the Pen Weight to 3 points **A**. The pointer currently looks like a pencil, which will allow you to draw the borders manually. Click, and draw a border under the first three cells **B**.

6. Change the Shading of Cells

By formatting one of the rows in our table, we can further highlight information. Highlight the ninth-row cells by clicking in the first cell and dragging to the right **A**. Next we'll change the color of the cells to make them look more like a dividing bar. Select the Table Tools Design tab and then choose the Table Styles group. Click on the shading menu, which looks like a paint bucket, and choose a dark shade of gray such as the Black, Text 1, Lighter 5% **B**. The row is now filled with a dark gray and clearly divides the total row from the earlier rows.

Year to Year Comparison

	FY '06	FY '07
Sales Revenue	$136.40	$165.30
Licensing Revenue	$34.20	$46.30
Dealer Fees	$24.40	$35.70
TOTAL REVENUE	$195.00	$247.30
Manufacturing	$87.40	$98.45
Marketing	$38.37	$56.35
TOTAL FEES	$125.77	$154.80
TOTAL	$69.23	$92.50

Year to Year Comparison

	FY '06	FY '07
Sales Revenue	$136.40	$165.30
Licensing Revenue	$34.20	$46.30
Dealer Fees	$24.40	$35.70
TOTAL REVENUE	$195.00	$247.30
Manufacturing	$87.40	$98.45
Marketing	$38.37	$56.35
TOTAL FEES	$125.77	$154.80
TOTAL	$69.23	$92.50

7. Adjust Size and Position

The table needs to be modified to fit on the page. In the first column, the words Licensing Revenue have wrapped onto two lines **A**. This creates a design anomaly as none of the other cells appear this way. You will want to correct irregular line breaks, as they disrupt the clean presentation of data; fix by adjusting the size of the table. Click the right edge of the table (be sure to click in the center where the cursor will change to a double arrow) and drag to the right until you reach the edge of the slide. Next click on an edge of the table (not on a handle) making sure that the cursor is a four way arrow. Click and drag to reposition the table on the slide. Position the table so it is optically centered between the left and right edges as well as between the space below the title and the bottom edge of the slide **B**. ▥

An Overview of Different Chart Types

Before you add a chart to your presentation, you should have a clear understanding of the many options you'll be presented with. PowerPoint 2007 offers 11 different categories and 73 unique chart styles. To the uninitiated (and even the savvy) this many choices can be truly intimidating. Let's take a look at some guiding principles for selecting the right chart type.

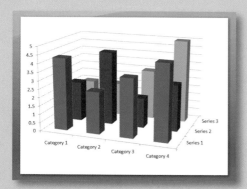

Column

The column chart is a popular option and is frequently used to present data that was arranged using rows or columns. This is very helpful for showing changes over time, such as figures that compare year-end financial results. The most common layout places categories of information along the horizontal axis, with the value entries falling along the vertical axis. PowerPoint offers several choices for column charts, including flat, 3-D, and pyramid shapes.

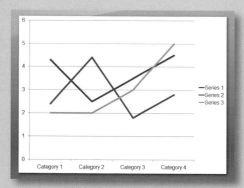

Line

Line charts are similar to column charts as they work well for data that is arranged in columns or rows in a worksheet. What differentiates them is that they can display continuous data over a range of time, which makes them excellent for showing trends. For a line chart to work properly, category data must be available in even increments (such as months or quarters), which are then spread along the horizontal axis. The value data is also evenly spread along the vertical axis. The points on the graph are then connected with a line; multiple colors can be used to illustrate multiple trends clearly.

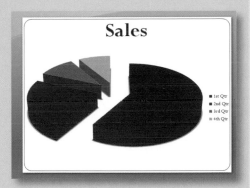

Pie

A pie chart works well to show the proportionate relationship of a single column or row to the whole. The chart represents the data series in proportionate sums, showing slice by slice what percentage of the whole pie is represented. The total of all the slice percentages comes to 100 percent. A pie chart works very well when the object of the chart is to show a relationship between entries (such as the results from a survey). Pie charts can be 2-D or 3-D depending upon the style of your slides.

> **T I P**
>
> **Better Pie Charts.** Be careful when creating pie charts so your graphic doesn't get too cluttered. Many more than eight categories, and you'll have a difficult-to-read chart. The same holds true if very many of the values are extremely small. For clarity, you can pull a section of a pie chart out to offset it and add emphasis.

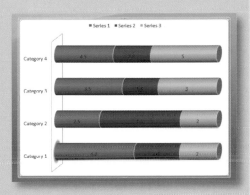

Bar

A bar chart can translate data from rows or columns into plotted bars. These are useful for comparing two or more individual items. The bar chart is a good option if you have long names for axis labels or if you are illustrating a value of duration. Options for creating bar charts include cylinder, cone, and pyramid.

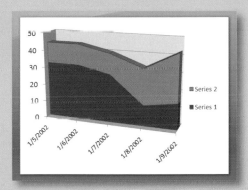

Area

Area charts can show data from rows and columns, and they are particularly well suited for showing the magnitude of change over time. An area chart can be used for showing financial or population growth, as it conveys both a change in individual value and a cumulative change in total value.

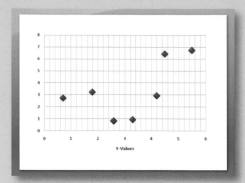

X Y (Scatter)

A scatter chart is a useful way to show the relationships among the values of a table. A scatter chart uses two-value axes, and uses number values on both the x- and y-axis. The data tends to be displayed in uneven intervals (hence "scattered") across the chart. The charts are most commonly used to show statistical or scientific data.

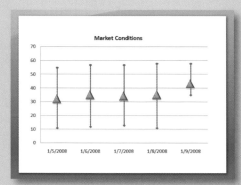

Stock

A stock chart is usually used to show the fluctuations of the stock market. It allows you to show information such as the High/Low and Close values of a specific stock. You have to organize the data in a particular order. Fortunately when you add the chart, the spreadsheet is already set up properly. To make sure the chart functions correctly, be careful not to modify the number of columns or the High/Low Close labels.

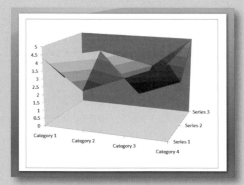

Surface

Surface charts can be difficult to read. They are most useful for displaying the optimum combinations between two sets of data. Colors and patterns are used to indicate areas that share the same range of values. Surface charts are often used to illustrate data like temperature readings. The chart is similar to the effect of wrapping a rubber sheet over a 3-D Column chart. In order to work properly, both categories and series data should be numeric values. A surface chart is not commonly used for financial and sales presentations; it is more useful to the scientific community. These charts are used to show relationships among large amounts of data that would otherwise be difficult to comprehend.

Doughnut

A doughnut chart, like a pie chart, shows the relationship of parts to a whole. Unlike a pie chart, it allows more than one column or row to be plotted. A doughnut chart is not the easiest to read, and is used far less frequently than other options like a stacked column or bar chart, which use the same principles.

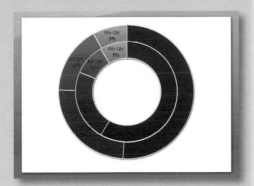

Bubble

A bubble chart is similar to a scatter chart. Your data must be listed so that x values appear in the first column and y values in the second. A third column (generally a percentage) is used to modify the size of the bubble. Bubble charts are not very common and are not always easily understood by audiences.

Radar

A radar chart can be used to compare the aggregate values of multiple data series from a table. A radar chart is a specialty chart and is not commonly used. ▥

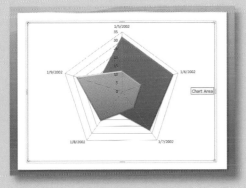

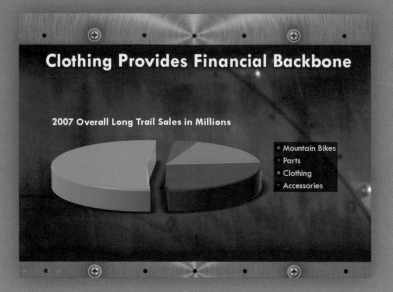

Building a Pie Chart

PowerPoint Makes Building and Stylizing a Pie Chart Simple

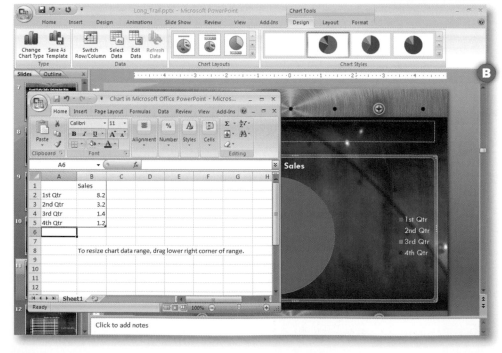

1. Insert a Chart

There are two main ways to create a dynamic chart in your presentation. You can go to the insert tab in the Ribbon and then click the Charts button in the Illustrations group. The Insert Chart window will appear and allow you to select a chart style. If the presentation template that you're using has a general content or chart placeholder, you can click the Charts icon to create your chart. To get started, click the slide 5 Thumbnail.

2. Insert a Pie Chart Placeholder

Slide 5 in your presentation will have a general-content placeholder that contains icons for Tables, Charts, SmartArt, Pictures, Clip Art, and Movies. Click the Insert Chart icon **A**. This will open up the Insert Chart window. Select the first thumbnail in the Pie group and click OK. A placeholder pie chart will be placed on the active slide as an Excel document simultaneously opens with placeholder content **B**. Click in the B1

	A	B	C	D	E
1		2007 Overall Long Trail Sales in Millions			
2	Mountain Bi	2.2			
3	Parts	3.2			
4	Clothing	6.4			
5	Accessories	0.5			
6	Other	1.5 **C**			

cell and modify the chart title to read, "2007 Overall Long Trail Sales in Millions." Modify A2–A6 to read Mountain Bikes, Parts, Clothing, Accessories, and Other. In Cells B2–B6, type in 2.2, 3.2, 6.4, 0.5, and 1.5 **C**. Now close the Excel document.

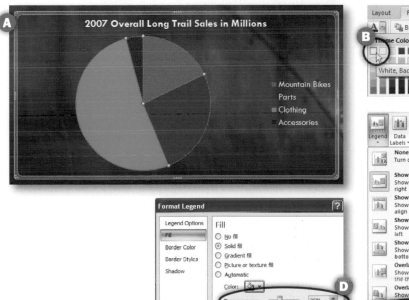

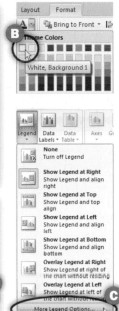

3. Modify the Inserted Chart

You'll notice that the text on the chart title and legend is hard to read. That's an easy fix. When selected, the chart will have a semi-transparent bounding box to let you know that it's active **A**. Click the Format tab in the Ribbon. In the WordArt Styles group, click the Text Fill button and select a white color swatch from the drop-down menu **B**. In the Layout tab, click the Legend drop-down menu in the Labels group and click More Legend Options **C**. Select the Fill button and then select Solid fill. Change your Color to black and your Transparency to about 35 percent **D**.

4. Add Emphasis with Titles

We need to draw attention to the fact that the Long Trail clothing line is outselling all other products. The first step is to direct the audience's attention to our specific agenda. By using a title like "Clothing Provides Financial Backbone," we guide our audience to a specific conclusion with our chart backing it up visually. Keep titles short and to the point. Imagine that you are writing newspaper headlines.

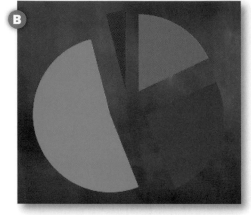

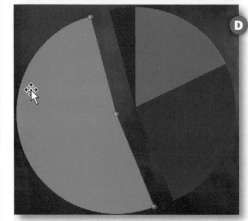

TIP

Nudging Objects. If you need to move an object just a tiny bit, then select the object and use the arrow keys. For even more precise control, hold down the Ctrl key and then use the arrow keys.

5. Add Emphasis with Explosions

Unless you have a license in pyrotechnics, we'll just use an exploded Pie chart. Click on your Pie chart and then click the Design tab in the Ribbon. Open up the Change Chart Type window by clicking the corresponding button in the Type group **A**. In the Pie group, click the Exploded Pie icon and then click OK. You'll notice that all of the pie pieces have exploded **B**. We just want to emphasize the clothing slice. Make sure all of the pieces are selected and then click the Layout tab. Click the Format Selection button in the current selection group. Adjust the Pie Explosion slider until it is at 0%, or closest to the Together label on the left **C**. Next, select just the Clothing (green) piece and pull it away from the rest of the pie **D**.

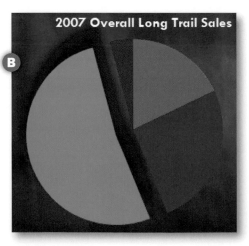

6. Add Dimension with a Drop-Shadow

With the Clothing piece still selected, click the Format tab in the Ribbon. Then click the Shape Effects drop-down menu in the Shape Styles Group. From this window you can select a drop-shadow preset or customize the shadow by selecting the Shadow Options button **A**. Select the Shadow Options button and then select Shadow in the Format Data Point window. Adjust your Shadow settings until the Clothing piece appears to float above the rest of the pie pieces **B**.

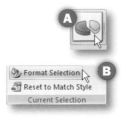

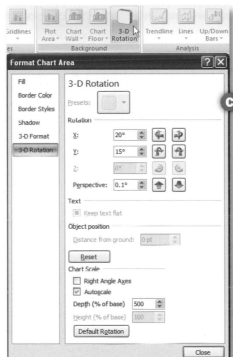

7. Convert Your Pie to 3-D

With your chart selected, click the Design tab, and then click the Change Chart Type button in the Type group. Select the Exploded pie in 3-D thumbnail and click OK **A**. You can also add to the 3-D look by clicking on the chart and then selecting the Format Selection button in the Current Selection group in the Format tab **B**. Click the 3-D Format button and experiment with different Bevels and Surfaces. To adjust the rotation and perspective, click the 3-D Rotation button in the Background group under the Layout tab and experiment with different options **C**. ▥

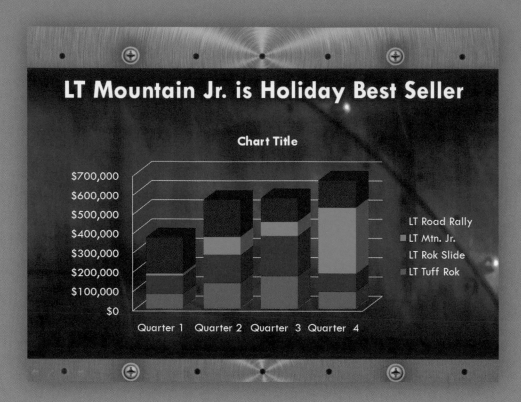

Building a Stacked Bar Chart

Using an Existing External Excel Chart in PowerPoint

	A	B	C	D	E
1		Quarter 1	Quarter 2	Quarter 3	Quarter 4
2	LT Tuff Rok	$74,345	$131,915	$167,912	$87,000
3	LT Rok Slide	$25,583	$146,819	$210,000	$95,000
4	LT Mtn. Jr.	$10,537	$91,894	$72,000	$341,000
5	LT Road Rall	$186,265	$192,760	$122,000	$141,000
6		$296,730	$563,388	$571,912	$664,000
7					

1. Start with an Existing Excel Chart
It's common to receive data in an Excel document that needs to be imported into a presentation. We'll take an existing Excel document and create a chart within Excel that can be pasted and modified in PowerPoint. To get started, open the Sales_by_Bike.xls Excel document in your Chapter 2 project folder, and select the chart data by clicking in cell A-1 and then shift-clicking in cell E-6.

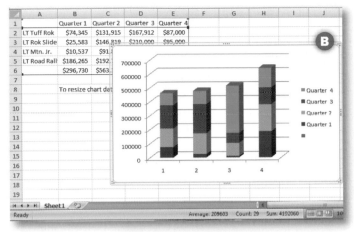

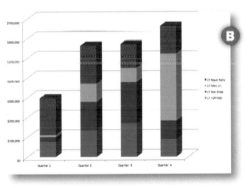

2. Convert to Chart

Click the Insert tab in the Ribbon and select the Column drop-down menu in the Charts group. Select the Stacked Column in the 3-D thumbnails in the 3-D Column group **A**. Excel will create a chart based on the existing data on sheet 1 in your document. Things may get a little confusing with the chart sitting right on top of your worksheet **B**. To move the chart to its own work sheet, select the chart and then click the Move Chart button in the design tab of your Ribbon. In the Move Chart window, select the New Sheet radio button and name your chart Sales by Bike and then click OK **C**. Your Sales by Bike chart will now reside on its own sheet.

3. Adjust Legends

You'll notice that the legends in your chart don't really explain exactly what you want them to. In the Design tab of your Ribbon, click the Switch Row/Column button in the Data group **A**. Now the chart correctly conveys total bike sales by quarter and what percentages of total sales were made up by each bike model **B**. Save your Excel worksheet.

4. Copy and Paste into PowerPoint

Select the chart in Excel and click the copy button in the Clipboard group within the Home tab **A**. Open the Ch2_Long_Trail_pptx presentation inside the Chapter 2 folder that you copied to your computer, and click the slide 8 Thumbnail. Click inside the content placeholder area on your slide and then click the Paste button in the Clipboard group of your Home tab **B**.

5. Adjust the Chart to Match Your Style

You'll notice that when it was pasted in, the chart retained the font style and chart style that were created in Excel. To modify the text quickly, simply click on the chart and select a thumbnail in the Chart Styles group under the Design tab in your Ribbon. Experiment with some of the other chart styles until you're satisfied with the result.

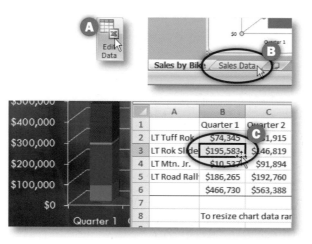

6. Adjust the Data

If you need to adjust the data, select the chart and click the Edit Data button in the Data group (within the Design tab) **A**. This will launch your Excel worksheet. It turns out that the LT Rok bike actually sold more than the data shows. Open up the data sheet by clicking the Sales Data tab at the bottom of your worksheet **B**. Select cell B-3 and enter $195,583. The change is then reflected in your PowerPoint chart **C**.

7. Chart Layout

Under the Design tab in your Power-Point application, you'll see that there are presets available in the Chart Layouts group **A**. Experiment with these until you've found a layout that fits your presentation. For more control over the chart layout, with the chart selected, click the Layout tab in your Ribbon. From inside this tab, you can control the Chart and Axis Titles, Data Labels, Axes, Gridlines, and more **B**.

8. Change Chart Type

The Change Chart Type button in the Design Tab is a powerful tool. Take a step back and put yourself in the shoes of your audience. If your message is that sales of the LT Mountain Jr. Bike really take off during the holidays, then maybe a 3-D Area Chart will illustrate that point more effectively. Select your chart and then click the Change Chart Type button in the Type Group under the Design tab. Select the 3-D Area thumbnail in the Area group **A**. Now your audience will be more aware of the dramatic sales spike for the LT Mountain Jr. in the fourth quarter **B**.

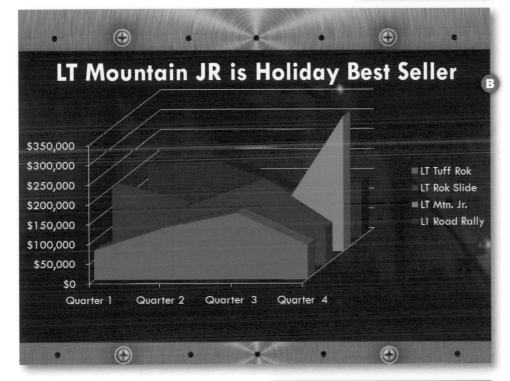

LT Mountain JR is Holiday Best Seller

- LT Tuff Rok
- LT Rok Slide
- LT Mtn. Jr.
- LT Road Rally

$350,000
$300,000
$250,000
$200,000
$150,000
$100,000
$50,000
$0

Quarter 1   Quarter 2   Quarter 3   Quarter 4

T I P

Make It Pop. To make the chart stand out from the background, stretch the chart's bounding box to the edges of your slide. In the Format tab, select a solid color in the Shape Fill drop-down menu by selecting the More Fill Colors button and adjust the transparency until your text and charts pop.

Highlights of SmartArt

One of the most powerful visual tools in PowerPoint is SmartArt. SmartArt makes it possible to enter and format text in an easy, clear, and visually pleasing graphic. These customizable, dynamic, built-in graphics will conform to your established look and help you decide quickly how to organize your information to emphasize your point.

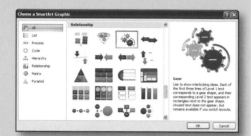

When to Use SmartArt

SmartArt will do most of the work for you when you have a slide with bullets or text that can be simplified or made more understandable within a graphic. If you're not really sure whether your data lends itself to a graphic, select the text and give it a try. SmartArt is the fastest and most elegant way to create a visual representation of anything from an organizational chart or decision tree to lists, processes, or matrixes. SmartArt should not be used to represent numerical data; it's best to use Charts for those.

Stacked Venn

Use to show overlapping relationships. A good choice for emphasizing growth or gradation. Works best with Level 1 text only. The first seven lines of Level 1 text correspond to a circular shape. Unused text does not appear, but remains available if you switch layouts.

A Comprehensive List

There are seven main categories in SmartArt: List, Process, Cycle, Hierarchy, Relationship, Matrix, and Pyramid. Within each category are several different ways of graphically representing your information. When you've decided upon a SmartArt category, browse through each chart style and click a thumbnail. PowerPoint will show you a larger color example and suggest when it's best to use each style.

Converting a List to a Graphic

One amazing feature of SmartArt is its ability to instantly convert an existing list to an attractive graphic. You can select your list in PowerPoint and then click the Convert to SmartArt Graphic button in the Paragraph group of your Home tab. A window will open, showing you the most common options available for your list. Roll over each thumbnail to view what your list might look like if it were converted to a particular style. If none of the styles appeal to you, you can always select the More SmartArt Graphics button.

Starting from Scratch

Many times you'll have a concept that you would like to explain graphically, but you're just not sure how to approach it. In the Insert Tab, click the SmartArt button in the Illustrations group. If you browse the gallery of SmartArt options, there is a good chance that you'll find an option to help illustrate your idea. Once you've identified a good match, select it and click OK. Now you can begin to modify the chart to match your goals.

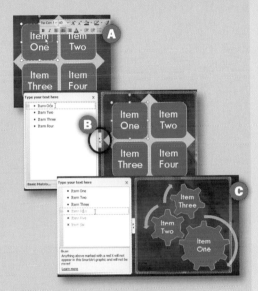

Entering Text Two Ways

There are two ways to enter text into a SmartArt graphic. One is to double-click directly into the text field and modify the text from within the graphic **A**. If you're used to a page layout or illustration program this will probably be the most intuitive. Another way is to click the arrows on the left of the SmartArt bounding box to reveal the Text pane **B**. Here you can enter text in a standard PowerPoint fashion. The Text pane has pre-determined fields that will populate your SmartArt graphic dynamically as you type. You'll notice that in some SmartArt choices red Xs instead of bullets will start to appear if you add too many items. This is because some SmartArt graphics can only contain a few fields (for instance, the Gear allows only three entries) **C**. If you really like the Gear or any other SmartArt graphic, remember that you can always add another graphic and modify it to work with the one that is already on the slide.

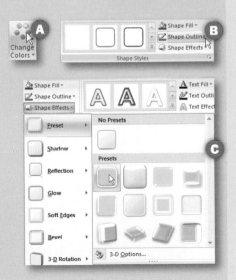

Mixing In a Little Style

Once you have the SmartArt graphic inserted into your slide that you think communicates your idea the best, you might want to mix in a little style. You can select your graphic and then modify the colors and style of illustration in the SmartArt Styles group under the Design tab. You'll find an assortment of color choices by selecting the Change Colors button **A**. Don't let those choices limit you. By selecting any of the graphical elements within a SmartArt Graphic, you can modify the color, transparency, and more in the Shape Styles group under the Format tab **B**. By clicking the Shape Effects button you'll find thumbnails that represent different illustrative style presets to choose from **C**. ⌨

> ### CAUTION
>
> **Too Much of a Good Thing.** Just because it's really easy to convert a list in PowerPoint into a graphic doesn't mean that you should do it for every list. If you want to add clarity or emphasize a list, convert it to SmartArt. If you have too many lists converted to SmartArt, then they will all blend together in the minds of the audience and lose their effectiveness.

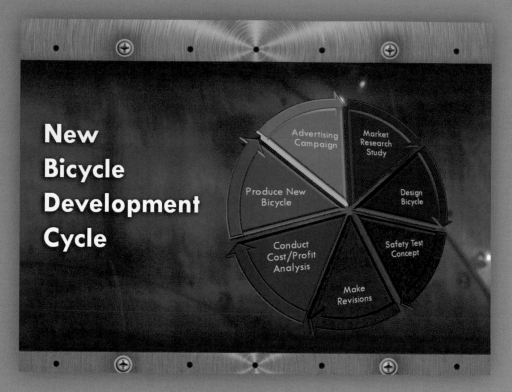

Working with SmartArt

Build an Attractive and Editable Informational Graphic

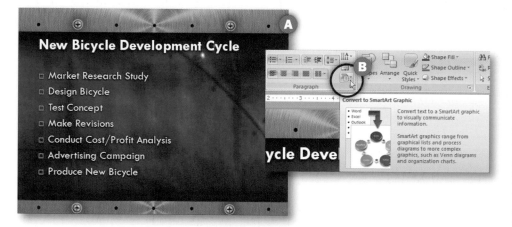

1. From Bullets to Graphics

Go to slide 9 in the Slides list. You'll notice that the headline says, "New Bicycle Development Cycle," but the slide is just a series of bullets. It doesn't suggest that the development process is repeated **A**. There is a quick way to remedy this problem: we can convert the bullets into a diagram. First, select all of the bulleted text. Then click the Home tab in the Ribbon. Hidden within the Paragraph group is a tiny icon called the Convert to SmartArt Graphic button **B**. Click the button once and a drop-down menu will appear. Roll over each thumbnail. You'll see how your bullets can be modified into several different diagrams.

2. Select the Right Template

To accurately portray the development cycle of a new bicycle, we want to make it clear that after a bicycle is produced, we continue to do market research and improve our products. We'll need to select a template that is cyclical. Click the Convert to SmartArt button again, and then select More SmartArt Graphics **A**. In the Cycle group, select the Segmented Cycle thumbnail and click OK **B**.

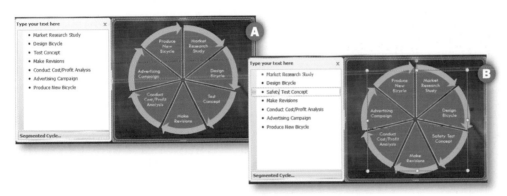

3. Make Text Edits

There are two ways to make a text edit to a portion of the diagram. One way is to double-click directly on the text and make the edit from within the diagram. Another approach is to open up the Text Pane and dynamically edit text or add text to your graphic **A**. If the Text pane is not open already, click the arrows to the left of your SmartArt bounding box. From within the Text Pane insert your cursor in front of Test Concept and add the word "Safety" **B**. Your diagram is dynamically updated with the text that you've entered.

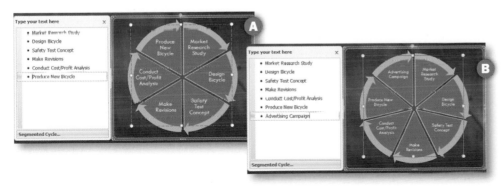

4. Add or Move Content

Select the bullet that says "Advertising Campaign" and delete it from your text pane **A**. SmartArt will dynamically resize the diagram to accommodate fewer steps in the process. Now place your cursor at the end of the last bullet and hit Enter. Type "Advertising Campaign" next to the bullet that you've just created. Your SmartArt diagram reflects the change immediately **B**.

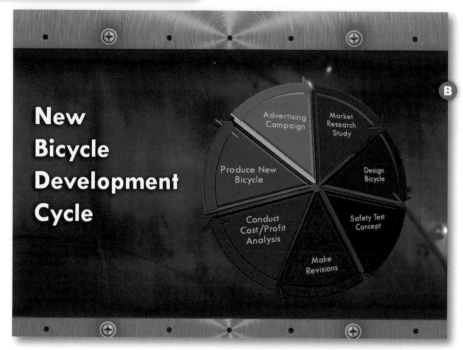

5. Add Dimension and Color

To add some dimension to your diagram, select the SmartArt graphic and then click the Design tab in the Ribbon. Click the More button at the bottom of the scroll bar in the SmartArt Styles group **A**. Slowly roll over the thumbnails to see how your diagram looks with different presets applied. Select a thumbnail that is close to what you are looking for and click it. Then select a color preset from the gallery that is available when you click the Change Colors button in the SmartArt Styles group **B**. 🎞

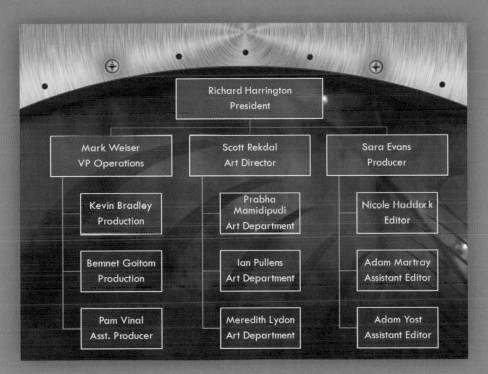

Building an Organizational Chart

An Organizational Chart Can Show the Makeup of a Company

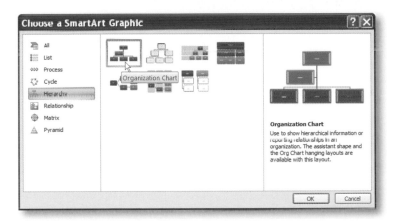

1. Access the Organizational Chart

PowerPoint 2007 brings many changes. One of those is the stand-alone Organizational Chart Maker that was used to create standard "org charts" for Office documents. The org chart (along with many other informational graphics) is now part of the SmartArt tools. Click on slide 10 to select an empty slide to hold the chart. Select the Insert tab in the Ribbon and from the Illustrations tab choose SmartArt. When the SmartArt window opens, choose the Hierarchy category and select Organizational Chart. Click OK to add the chart.

2. Modify the Organizational Chart Structure

Unless your company has the exact number of employees as the default layout, you'll likely need to modify the SmartArt graphic. In the case of this Organizational Chart, you will modify it to have one box on top, followed by three subordinates who each have three subordinates who report to them. Select the second box on the slide and then press delete to remove it.

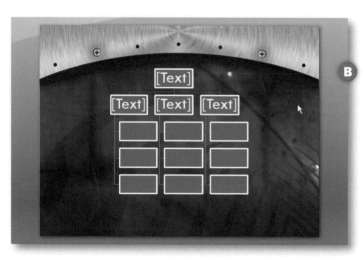

3. Add Subordinates

Select the first box in the second row so it is active (click on the outer border). From the SmartArt Tools Design tab choose Layout in the Create Graphic group. Set the layout to Right Hanging (this will add boxes in a vertical column below the manager box) **A**. Click the Add Shape button in the Create Graphic group three times to add three subordinates. Switch to the next manager and repeat the Right Hanging layout and Add Shape commands. Repeat for the third manager as well **B**.

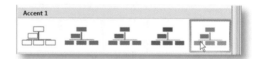

4. Adjust the Size and Style of the Chart

The SmartArt graphic can be much better sized, positioned, and styled to fit in with the overall design of this presentation. Click and pull the corners of the SmartArt box to size and position it on the page. Next, from the SmartArt Tools Design tab click the Change Colors button. Set the chart to a contrasting color, such as the Transparent Gradient Range from the Accent 1 category.

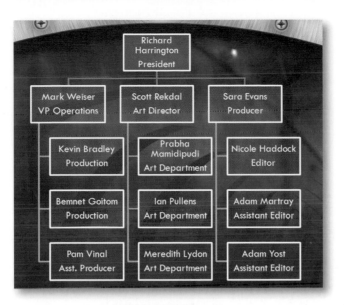

5. Enter Data into the Chart

Once your chart is built, it is time to populate it with information. Click in the [Text] block in the first box to add type; you can enter your own data or use the information below to fill in the chart. After typing a name, you can press Enter to add a title.

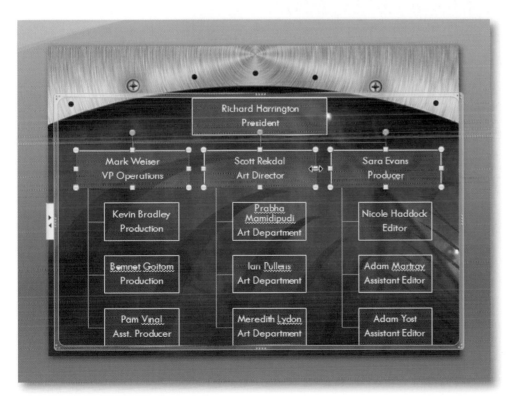

6. Adjust Size for Optical Clarity

In order to improve the layout, you can increase the amount of space between each column. One of the easiest ways to do this is to increase the size of the boxes. Drag the side handles of the top box so the text fits on two lines. Next click on the first box in the second row; then hold down the shift key and click on the other two (so all three boxes are actively selected). Then click and drag an edge handle on one of the second-row boxes to make it bigger. All three boxes will resize and make the columns appear cleaner. ▦

3

PHOTOS & GRAPHICS

Selecting & Preparing Images for Your Presentation

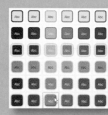

KNOWING WHAT TYPES of images to use and how to make them motivate, educate, and stimulate your audience is a powerful weapon to have in your arsenal. We've all suffered through unimaginative presentations with mismatched clip art and poorly handled photos. The end result is usually an audience that walks away missing the point or is simply too bored to care.

Raster Versus Vector

There are two major categories of graphics—raster and vector. Knowing the difference (as well as the pros and cons of each) will help you make smart choices. In a nutshell, here's what you need to know.

Raster graphics are generally built with a matrix of picture elements (pixels). Raster graphics (also called bitmaps) generally describe those images that originated from sources like digital cameras, scanners, or screen captures. They are well suited for photographic images. There are several formats for raster graphics, including Windows Bitmap and JPEG.

Vector graphics are created by using points, lines, or other geometric objects. A vector graphic can generally be scaled to a very large size with no loss of quality. Additionally, the files usually require very little disk space. Vector graphics are well suited for illustrations, and usually they will retain their shape and transparency when imported into PowerPoint. Graphics with transparency will allow the background of your slide to show through. Typical formats for vector graphics are .wmf and .eps.

Making Clip Art Your friend

Ask a designer to incorporate clip art into a design and it might induce a gag reflex. There is good news however; clip art has come a long way, and if you know how to find the good stuff and use it properly, you can take an ordinary presentation and make it look posh and

sophisticated. PowerPoint includes a large library of clip art to choose from as well as a series of AutoShapes that can turn a hard-to-follow concept in to a visual *a-ha!* Being able to guide your audience with visual clues can reinforce your objectives as long as you know how to use them, when to use them, and which ones to use.

Using Photos in Your Presentations

With the prevalence of affordable high-quality digital cameras and scanners it is easier than ever to integrate photos in your presentations. PowerPoint gives you a wide array of tools to compress, resize and manipulate photos; giving you the power you need. With all that power comes great responsibility. Learning how to optimize your photos for portability and performance will make your presentations run better on a variety of different systems and allow you to be able to e-mail documents that once could only be burned to a CD.

Understanding File Formats

As you work with digital photos, clip art, and graphics from the Internet, you'll come across a lot of different image types. Several different file formats have been created for both special purposes and licensing reasons. Without any additional work on your part, Microsoft PowerPoint 2007 recognizes the following options.

picture.wmf

Windows Metafile (.emf or .wmf)

This file format is a proprietary one made by Microsoft for use throughout their software products. You will find it commonly used in the Microsoft Clip Organizer for illustrations. The .wmf file type was introduced first and supports 16 bits of information. The .emf file format (also known as enhanced metafile) is newer, and supports 32 bits of information for higher visual quality.

picture.bmp

Windows Bitmap (.bmp, .dib, or .rle)

This file format is commonly used by Windows and is generally very compatible across applications. A disadvantage is that the files are typically not compressed, which can result in a large file size. When PowerPoint gets to a slide with graphics on it, it must cache the graphic. This can result in delays during your presentation when you're clicking to advance slides. Most users prefer to work with compressed formats like JPEG when they need to insert photos.

Computer Graphics Metafile (.cgm)

The use of CGM files became a standard in 1987, they can be used for both vector and raster graphics. It is not widely supported for use on the Internet, but is more prevalent in technical fields like engineering. You may likely encounter it as well for military uses. CGM files generally are small.

GIF—Graphics Interchange Format (.gif)

The GIF format (pronounced gif or jif) is a very common Web format. It was originally developed for use in the CompuServe online service. The files are limited to a maximum of 256 colors (referred to as a bit image). This limit of colors can reduce file size, but can be problematic for photos. Users will choose GIFs for two primary reasons: the need for embedded transparency (such as in a corporate logo) or for basic animation.

JPEG—Joint Photographic Experts Group (.jpg)

picture.jpg

The JPEG format is used to optimize large photos for multimedia use, such as the Internet or a slide presentation. The format uses lossy compression, which means that data is permanently thrown away to reduce file sizes. Most point-and-shoot digital cameras also use JPEG images. The JPEG format is best suited for images with many colors, such as photographs. But keep in mind a JPEG file suffers quality loss every time it is modified and resaved. Many professional image editors will wait to create a JPEG file until they have completed their image-editing tasks.

PNG—Portable Network Graphics (.png)

Picture.png

The PNG file format merges the best features of JPEG and GIF files. It allows for a 24-bit image (millions of colors) plus embedded transparency. While not all Web browsers support it (notably older versions of Internet Explorer) it is a standardized Web graphics format. PNG graphics are well suited for presentations, especially if you need embedded transparency.

PICT—Macintosh PICT (.pct)

picture.pct

This is the original image format used by Macintosh computers (pre-OS X). It can be used for both raster and vector graphics. This format will likely be encountered if you are working with an older PowerPoint presentation created on a Mac. While the format is widely supported, it is becoming less common.

TIFF—Tagged Image File Format (.tif)

picture.tif

The TIFF format is commonly used for high-quality printing. It can store up to 48 bits of color information, making it very accurate. TIFFs can be quite large is size, but they do support compression to reduce the size of the file.

TIP

Do Not Copy & Paste Images. If you copy and paste an image into a presentation, PowerPoint will attempt to link the image. It is a much better idea to save the file to a disk and choose the Insert Tab and click the Picture button.

CAUTION

CMYK Conversion. Many TIFF files are formatted using the CMYK image mode (Cyan Magenta Yellow and blacK), which is used in professional printing. This can cause problems in PowerPoint. It is a good idea to ask the image provider for an image using the RGB mode (Red Green Blue). You can also convert the images yourself with free converter applications such as Irfanview (www.irfanview.com).

Vector Markup Language (.vml)

Vector Markup Language (VML) is based on an XML exchange. It is an emerging standard and is supported by newer Web browsers. The standard is being pushed by Microsoft and the W3C, the standards setting consortium on the Web.

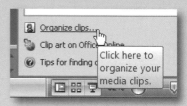

Other Formats

There are many other file formats that you'll likely encounter, especially if you work with graphic professionals or Adobe applications. You have two options to work around unsupported image formats.

The first is to use the Microsoft Clip Organizer to import and convert the files. You can access the Clip Organizer by selecting the Insert tab then clicking the Clip Art button. The Clip Art pane opens to the right of your slide. Click the Organize clips button at the bottom of the pane to open the Microsoft Clip organizer. Microsoft installs several filters to convert images to acceptable formats for use in Microsoft Office.

If the Clip Organizer cannot import the image, then you must use another piece of software to convert the images. Nearly every other software shares file formats in common with PowerPoint (especially JPEG files). You can go back to the original application (or the image creator) to get another file. If that doesn't work, then download an affordable image converter like Irfanview (www.irfanview.com) for PCs or Graphic Converter (www.lemkesoft.com) for Macintosh. ▦

Sizing and Optimizing Photos

Accurately Scale and Crop Your Photos to Fit the Page and Optimize the File Size

1. Prepare Your Files

In order to complete this exercise (and others in this chapter) you'll need to copy the project files to your local computer. From the project CD-ROM, open the HTW Project Files folder and copy the Chapter 3 folder to your local hard drive. This folder contains all of the files needed for this chapter. Open the file Ch3_Independence.pptx and switch to slide 2.

2. Add the First Photo

There are many ways to add an image to a slide. Lets examine one of the easiest. Select the Insert tab from the Ribbon. Click the Picture button to insert a photo from a file **A**. Navigate to the Chapter 3 folder you copied to your hard drive and open up the Photos folder. Select the first image, 01 Hall and click Insert. The photo is added to your slide; however it needs to be rotated and scaled **B**.

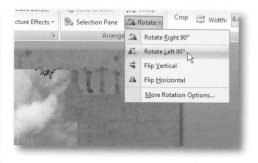

3. Adjust Rotation and Size

In order for the photo to display correctly, it must be rotated 90 degrees counterclockwise. Click the Format tab to adjust the image. In the Arrange group, click Rotate and choose Rotate Left 90° to properly orient the photo. Next, click and drag on the sizing handle in the upper right corner to adjust the size of the image.

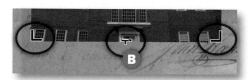

4. Crop the Image

With the image still selected we can further refine it. By cropping, we can remove the crowd from the bottom of the photo. In the Ribbon, click the Format tab. In the Size group, click the Crop button **A**. Cropping handles appear on each corner and edge. You can drag these to hide part of the photo. Click the bottom edge and drag upward to crop the tourists out of the shot **B**.

5. Position the Image

Move your mouse over the center of the image until the cursor changes into a four-way arrow. Click and drag to reposition the photo on the slide.

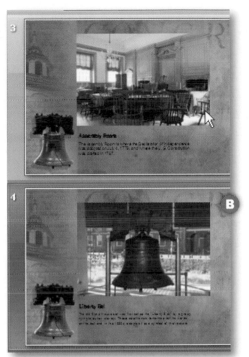

6. Use an Image Placeholder

Some slide templates (including this one) use placeholders. A placeholder "reserves" a spot for an image or text in a slide design. A placeholder does not show up during a slide show if it's left empty. However, it is easy to see when laying out the slide. Select slide 3 in the Slides tab of this project. Click the Image Placeholder icon in the middle of the slide **A**. The Insert Picture window opens up; navigate to the Photos folder you accessed earlier and select 02 Assembly Room. Click Insert to add the photo to the slide. Switch to slide 4 and insert the photo 03 Bell onto the slide **B**.

TIP

When to Optimize. Optimization works best when you are finished with a presentation. Once images are optimized, it's difficult to enlarge or modify them without a loss of quality. You should choose to optimize a copy of your presentation before you try to move it onto a portable drive or laptop to give a presentation.

7. Optimize Your Digital Images

Digital photos are typically larger than you need for a slide. For example, a 7-megapixel digital camera will capture an image that is nearly 3,000 pixels wide. This is approximately three times larger than what you need in a standard 1024 x 768 presentation. That extra file size bloats a presentation, taking more disk space and more time to load. You can avoid image bloat with compression. From the Format tab, click Compress Pictures. Click the Options... button to specify optimization for Print, Screen, or E-mail. Click OK and Apply the optimization when you are ready. ▨

Using Clip Art

Clip art can work for or against you depending on how you use it. Making sure that your selections are consistent with the look of your presentation (colors, style, and overall feeling) is essential. You won't always be able to find exactly what you're looking for, but there are ways to edit clip art within PowerPoint to adapt it to your specific needs.

Browsing Clip Art

When you installed your Microsoft Office software, a library of clip art was included in the install. Microsoft has also made additional clip art collections available online (you'll have access to them within PowerPoint if you are connected to the Internet). To browse through the available clip art selections, click on the Insert tab in the Ribbon. Then click on Clip Art in the Illustrations group. The Clip Art palette will open on your right. Use the search box to locate your illustration. You can drag and drop the thumbnail onto your slide or click on the Clip Art thumbnail to insert it on the current slide.

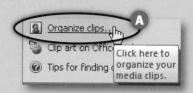

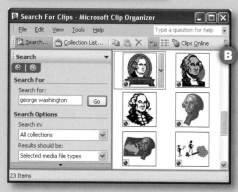

Expanding the Clip Art Library

Once the Clip Art palette is open, click the Organize clips icon **A**. The Microsoft Clip Organizer will launch, displaying a collections list on the left and a viewing pane on the right **B**. It is important that you keep similar topics and styles together by creating new folders for each. To add a new folder to your existing library, click File, then New collection. Once the folder has been created and named, click File, then Add Clips to Organizer. You can then add clips automatically (your drive will be searched for all media files and a shortcut will be created in your Clip Organizer, leaving the originals in place) or select On My Own or From Scanner or Camera. If you have a scanner or camera hooked up, the Clip Organizer will launch the appropriate driver to pull your images in. There are also a variety of other clip art resources available online; www.iStockphoto.com is a great resource for clip art, photos, flash animations, and video.

> ### INSIGHT
>
> **On My Own.** It's usually best to use the On My Own option to add clips to your Clip Organizer. You can create folders for specific styles and categories within the organizer and then populate the folders with only the images, movies, and sounds that you know will be useable. It's like organizing your closet—although the parachute pants are great for break dancing, it's best to leave them out of your regular wardrobe rotation.

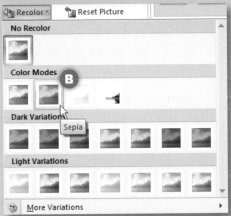

Modifying Clip Art

To maintain consistency within a presentation, many times it is necessary to modify the original colors or style of an illustration. You can make these adjustments by clicking on your clip art, and you'll see a red tab in the Ribbon called Picture Tools. Click the Format tab beneath it. From the Adjust group, click Recolor **A**. Roll your cursor over the different options until you find a style that matches your presentation **B**. Can't find what you're looking for in the presets? Click More Variations. ▦

T I P

Selecting the Right Clip Art. Often a presentation is created using text, and then clip art is selected to match each slide. That workflow is ok, as long as you are consistent with the style of clip art that you select, and that style is consistent with your overall graphic look. For example, if you are using a woodcut style of clip art on most of your presentation, don't suddenly integrate a watercolor style of clip art just because it fits the text better.

T I P

Raster/Vector Resources. Looking for more news and information on computer graphics? Then don't miss our blog and resource Web site at www.rastervector.com.

AutoShapes

Organizing Information Visually Helps Guide Your Audience Through the Messages

1. When to Use a Shape

When manipulated to match the design of your overall presentation, AutoShapes can not only visually organize information but can add the professional polish that will set you apart. To get started, select slide 5.

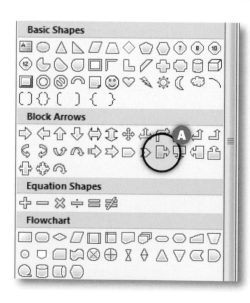

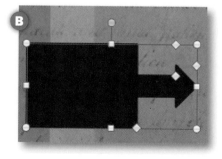

2. Draw a Shape

You'll find the Shapes icon under the Insert tab in the Illustrations group. Click on the icon and select any shape from the drop-down menu **A**. Your cursor will change to crosshairs. Click and drag the mouse to create the shape that you selected. Release the mouse button when you are satisfied with the size of the shape **B**. To constrain proportions, hold down the Shift key while dragging your mouse. The shape will remain editable if you want to resize it later.

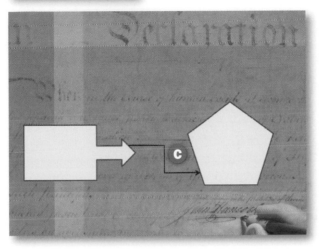

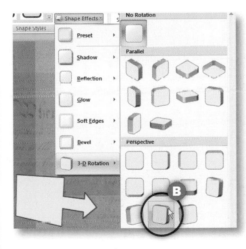

3. Create a Simple Diagram

Create another shape on the opposite side of the page. Now select a line shape **A**. With your cursor still in the crosshairs mode, hover over one of the shapes you've created until the edges of the shape are highlighted with series of small red boxes **B**. Click and drag the mouse to the shape that you would like to connect to. Release the mouse button when you are satisfied with the position of the connecting line **C**.

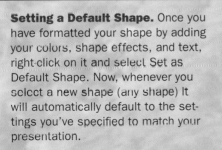

4. Modify Shapes to Match Your Design

Click on a shape that you've created. Under the Drawing Tools tab, select the Format tab and click on the Shape Effects drop-down menu **A**. Roll over a few presets and your shape will display a live preview **B**. It is possible to add images within a shape; add textures; move the shape around in 3-D space; make the shape appear to be made of glass; adjust the opacity, direction, distance, and softness of a drop shadow; add simple or beveled 3-D text within a shape, and more. Experiment with the different options available to you. ▥

Preparing Logos with Transparency

Having a Logo with Transparency Allows for Easy Integration

1. Limitations
The Set Transparent Color tool will work very well if the logo that you are manipulating has a solid-color background. If the background you are trying to make transparent has a pattern or gradient, this method will only set one color to be transparent, leaving all other colors visible in the images background. To get started, select slide 6.

2. Import Logo File
In the Ribbon, click the Insert tab. From the Illustrations group, click the picture icon. Navigate to the Chapter 3 folder that you copied to your computer. Open the Photos folder and select the file 04 American History Logo.jpg. Click the Insert button at the bottom of the window to insert. You'll notice that the logo imported with a blue, rectangular background that doesn't quite match the look of the presentation.

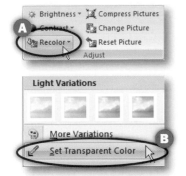

3. Make the Background Transparent

Select the logo that you've just imported. In the Ribbon under Picture Tools, select the Format tab. From the Adjust group, click the Recolor icon **A**. Click the Set Transparent Color button **B**. With the Set Transparent Color tool activated, select the solid blue background of the American History logo. The logo should now have a mostly transparent background **C**.

4. Work with Jagged Edges

You'll notice that there is a slightly jagged blue edge around the logo **A**. This effect is called aliasing, and it's a common issue with this method of making the background transparent. However, it's easy to disguise. Click the Format tab in the Ribbon, select the Picture Effects button, and scroll down to Glow **B**. In the Glow Variations window, select accent color 3, 8 pt Glow. This will ensure an appropriate glow size to disguise the aliasing issue **C**. Then select the More Glow Colors button at the bottom of the window and choose a golden yellow color. There still will be some remnants of the former background color if you look closely, but this method should effectively disguise the aliasing problem from anyone viewing the presentation **D**. 🖮

T I P

Working with Multiple Logos. Many times you will want to have a slide in your presentation that includes multiple logos in a variety of colors. A way to maintain the overall visual style of your presentation is to place them in a table. Make sure that the table uses colors that are consistent with your presentation. It's usually best to use a white background in order to accommodate the largest variety in colors.

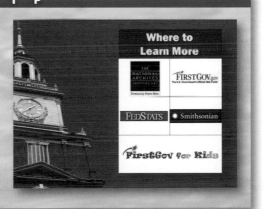

Acquiring Images with Digital Cameras & Scanners

You'll often need to bring original photos into your presentation. These may come from photos you take with a digital camera or from a flatbed scanner. It is important to understand how these devices treat digital images and to know how to import them into Microsoft PowerPoint.

Digital Cameras

ISTOCKPHOTO/LONG HA

The good news is that most digital cameras can take a picture large enough for use in a presentation. However, you'll want to look for cameras with features like a good lens and a flash to help you take better pictures. Besides camera quality, there are three major issues to consider when working with a digital camera:

- *Transfer of Images*—Be sure to load the drivers required for your hardware. If you work with several different cameras, you may want to get a USB card reader that supports multiple formats.

- *Image Size*—Most digital photos are much larger than you'll need for a presentation. This is because images are generally intended for print output. You can use the Compress Pictures command (see Sizing and Optimizing Photos) or an image editor like Adobe Photoshop or Photoshop Elements.

- *File Format*—Digital cameras usually write files to one of three formats. JPEG, TIFF, or a camera raw format. PowerPoint can read JPEG or TIFF files for use in a presentation. Camera raw files will need to be converted.

Flatbed Scanners

ISTOCKPHOTO/HEIKO ETZRODT

A scanner allows you to convert photos or documents into digital images. Doing this can be useful for inserting photos that were shot on film and printed or printed items like a newspaper story. There are several scanners available that are reasonably priced (in the $99 range). Be sure to look for one that has a minimum optical resolution of 300 pixels per inch.

Older versions of PowerPoint offered an Insert From Scanner command. This would scan the image and insert it directly into your slide. This could lead to bloated files, however, so Microsoft decided to leave it out of the current release. In PowerPoint 2007, the recommended workflow is to scan images directly to a disk and save them as files (JPEGs or TIFFs work best). ⌨

Creating a Photo Album

This Quick and Easy System Creates a Professional-Looking Photo Album

1. Insert a Photo Album

A photo album can hold multiple images on a single slide. In the Ribbon, click the Insert tab. From the Illustrations group, click the Photo Album icon and select New Photo Album.

2. Import Your Photos

Select Insert picture from: File/Disk button and navigate to the Chapter 3 folder that you copied to your computer. Select the Photos folder and then the 05 Album_Photos folder. Click in an empty area of the window and drag around all of the photo thumbnails in the folder. You'll notice that the filenames for all of the images that you selected are now in the Pictures in Album Window.

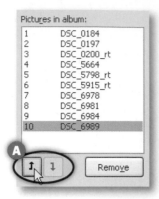

3. Organize Your Photos

Click on a filename in the Pictures in album window and it will appear in the adjacent Preview window. You can specify the order of the photos in your album by selecting a photo and using the up and down arrow keys beneath the Pictures in album window to rearrange their order **A**. If a photo needs to be rotated (such as image 7 DSC_0197), then select its filename and rotate it using the rotate clockwise or rotate counterclockwise buttons **B**.

T I P

Selecting Multiple Images. Select multiple images in the Pictures in Album window by shift-clicking adjacent filenames or by control (Ctrl) clicking separated file names.

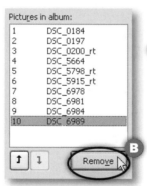

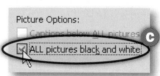

4. Review and Adjust

Click on each filename In the Pictures in album window and adjust the brightness and contrast levels using the buttons below the Preview window **A**. Remove any duplicates or unwanted photos by selecting the filename and clicking the Remove button below the Pictures in album window **B**. Many times there will be a variety of different styles of photography or a wide range of colors. To make the entire album consistent with the historic approach of this presentation, select the ALL pictures black and white option **C**.

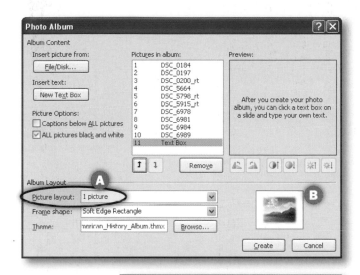

5. Utilize Album Layout

Click on Picture Layout and select 1 picture. This will center each photo on its own page **A**. Select Soft Edge Rectangle from the Frame shape drop-down menu. This will give each photo a feathered edge to help blend into the slide background. Look at the thumbnail representation to the right **B**. In the Theme menu click Browse. Navigate to the Sources folder inside the Chapter 3 folder that you copied to your computer. Select American_History_Album.thmx. If you would like to add a slide with a blank text box, there is also a New Text Box button to accommodate that. You'll notice that if you select it, a new number will appear in your Pictures in album window titled Text Box.

INSIGHT

Why Can't I Change My Frame Shape? If your Picture Layout is set to Fit to Slide, the picture will occupy the entire slide and not allow any Frame Shape adjustments. To allow these adjustments, simply make the picture anything other than Fit to Slide.

6. Create and Modify

Click the Create button at the bottom of the window and let PowerPoint go to work **A**. A photo album is automatically created to the specifications that you selected **B**. Even though PowerPoint has automated this process, all of your photos remain editable. You can still click on them and make modifications using the Format tab. You can also cut and paste these slides into your main presentation. ▦

Adding Custom Borders

Borders can often help a photo or text box stand out from the background or other photos on a page. There are a few different ways to approach borders and frames.

Adding a Border

Adding Impact with Visual Style

Select a photo or shift- click on multiple photos that you would like to modify with a border. Under Picture Tools in the Rib-bon, select the Format tab. In the Picture Styles group, click the Picture Border drop-down menu **A**. From here you can choose the color, line weight, and style of your border. This is a simple way to help your photos stand out from the background or to make a series of different photos tie together visually **B**.

Select a photo or shift-click on multiple photos that you would like to modify with a touch of visual style. Under Picture Tools in the Ribbon, select the Format tab. In the Picture Styles group, there is a series of thumbnails with a variety of different framing/style options to select from. With your photos still selected, roll over each option and watch what happens to your photos. PowerPoint will give you a live preview of several different frames and overall photo styles to choose from. Be patient, some computers are faster than others at rendering a live preview.

Keeping Visuals Consistent

Although it may be fun to have a different border or frame for each photo, it is more visually appealing to have a consistent color and style to all of your borders and frames. The focus should always be on the content, not the carrier. Your audience should be focusing on your images, and not anticipating what kind of border you'll use next.

Using Borders and Text Boxes

Borders and shape styles can be used to modify text boxes to add emphasis **A**. The process of modifying text boxes is very similar to modifying picture boxes. Just select the text box that you would like to manipulate and click the Format tab beneath the Drawing Tools tab. You can now roll over different styles in the Shape Styles gallery and review the live preview of your text box modifications **B**. Be cautious about making font and color changes that do not match your overall design. ▦

T I P

Quick Access to Picture Styles.
The Quick Access Toolbar is a customizable toolbar that allows you to have access to functions that are independent of the tab that is currently active. Right-click one of the thumbnail icons in the Picture Styles Gallery. Select Add Gallery to Quick Access Toolbar. Voila! Now you'll always have access to your style Gallery.

Enhancing Photo Appearance with PowerPoint

PowerPoint Allows for the Enhancement of Images to Improve Exposure and Contrast

1. Adjust an Image

Within PowerPoint, you can perform minor image touchups to improve a photo. This is a convenient and fast way to fix an image that's not quite right. To make things easier, select slide 7, which has an exterior photo of Independence Hall already on it. Click on the photo to select it.

2. Improve the Image

The image is a bit dark. PowerPoint gives you two controls to adjust images: Brightness brightens (or darkens) the image; Contrast increases (or decreases) the intensity of the blacks. Click the Format tab in the Ribbon, and then click the Brightness or Contrast buttons in the Adjust group. Increase Brightness to taste, then restore any unwanted image lightening with the Contrast slider. █

Give and Take. If you add brightness, you'll often need to increase contrast to achieve the image's best appearance. As brightness increases, the shadow areas will wash out, which required contrast to be intensified. If you'd like to adjust both properties simultaneously, then choose Picture Correction Options from either the Brightness or Contrast menus. For this image, add 20 percent to both the Brightness and Contrast fields.

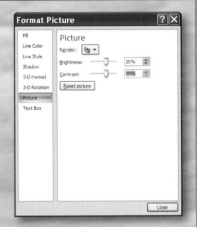

Go Pro with Adobe Photoshop or Adobe Photoshop Elements. While fixing images in PowerPoint is convenient, there's a world of improved opportunities to enhance images using a dedicated image editor. There are many different ones, but the market leaders are Adobe Photoshop and its scaled down counterpart, Photoshop Elements. If you plan to work regularly with photos, one of these is an important investment to make. For most users, the moderately priced Photoshop Elements ($99) will suffice. While PowerPoint offers only two commands for improving images (Brightness and Contrast), Photoshop Elements offers more than 100. Despite the number of features, the program is intuitive and truly useful. We'll explore Photoshop features occasionally throughout this book. If you want to learn more, check out one of Rich's books on Photoshop (he has several).

4

AUDIO/VIDEO & MULTIMEDIA

*Integrating Sound
and Motion into
Your Presentation*

I T HAS BECOME increasingly more common to see audio and video files integrated into PowerPoint presentations. Whether it's a music track to set the mood or sound effects to add emphasis, a videotaped product demonstration or an animation to capture the audience's attention, effective use of audio/video and multimedia will ensure that your presentation stimulates your audience.

Understanding File Formats

Just because you can open a file on your computer does not mean that Power-Point can play it back. While the operating system turns to the Windows Media Player or Web browser plug-ins, Power-Point is a more closed system. In order for a file to play back in a slide show, the Windows Media Player Interface has to recognize the file. Unfortunately, the list of supported file formats is not long. It is important to have a thorough understanding of what will and won't play inside of PowerPoint.

Using Audio and Video

When using an audio or video file, there are several considerations, from technical challenges like having the file properly sized or compressed to stickier issues like copyright. It is important to realize that audio and video files can greatly impact the size (and stability) of a presentation.

One of the greatest challenges when working with media files is codecs. Codec is a compound word that means a compressor/decompressor, and it is an extension that adds capability to your computer. Codecs run from very

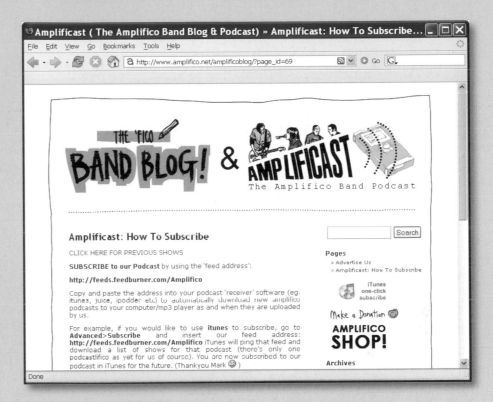

common ones like Cinepak or MPEG-1 to custom-installed ones such as DivX. It is important that your media files and related technology be thoroughly tested on all machines that you intend to use for playback of the presentation.

Controlling File Playback

While there's nothing up to the level of a universal remote control, you do have great flexibility in controlling your media files. You can set them up to start automatically or you can add buttons for common tasks like start and stop. Additionally, you can set an audio file to continue playing across multiple slides in a presentation. Once you understand the

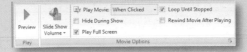

many ways that media can be played within a presentation, you can begin to effectively integrate media into your own presentations.

Integrating Web Pages and Multimedia

You'll often need to bring the Internet into your presentation. It's important to be able to link to live Web content as well as embed static Web content. Live content is helpful, as it allows you to explore the Internet and include the latest information in your presentation. But static content allows for a safety net when an Internet connection is unavailable.

So whatever your media needs are, you'll benefit from this chapter. Let's get started on the path to media-rich presentations.

Supported Audio File Formats

There are a lot of competing audio formats out there. Microsoft PowerPoint 2007 recognizes the following options without any additional work on your part. The easiest solution is to stick with one of these formats whenever possible.

Sound.aif

AIFF—Audio Interchange File Format (.aiff or .aif)

This is the sound file format originally used on Apple and Silicon Graphics (SGI) computers. The audio files are stored in an 8-bit monaural (mono or one channel) format, which is not compressed. AIFF files can contain two channels (16-bit) and carry stereo sound. This format leads to large file sizes, and can usually be avoided in favor of more efficient files like an MP3, which balances audio quality with file size.

Sound.au

AU Audio—UNIX Audio (.au)

This file format is a common format used for UNIX computers. While the format is supported by PowerPoint, there are no advantages to using it.

Sound.mid

MIDI file—Musical Instrument Digital Interface (.mid or .midi)

This file format is very old, and was originally designed for the interchange of musical information between musical instruments, synthesizers, and computers. Unless you have robust musical instruments hooked up to your computer, you might as well forget this one. MIDI files will generally sound like bad cell phone ringtones when played on a personal computer.

Sound.mp3

MP3—MPEG-1 Audio Layer 3 (.mp3)

This is a popular and common sound file format that you will likely encounter on the Internet. This efficient file is cross-platform compatible, has a clean sound and small size. It is a very common file format and has been a standard since 1991. This is a good file format to use because of its compatibility and quality.

Sound.wav

Windows Audio file—Wave Form (.wav)

This audio file format is a holdover from the early days of digital audio on Windows computers. The file format is generally cross-platform, and stores sounds as waveforms. There are several different compression options, which allow for the audio to be stored at different quality settings. Because of its large file sizes, which can bloat your presentation, this format is not very popular.

T I P

Need to Embed. If you want the audio file to embed into the presentation, use a WAV file. All other formats can only be linked.

Sound.wma

WMA file—Windows Media Audio (.wma)

This is an audio file that has been compressed using one of the Microsoft Windows Media Audio codecs. If users extract audio from a CD using Windows Media Player or Windows Media Encoder, they are likely to store the audio file this way. The WMA codecs have several versions, so it's important to test your files on all playback machines. If possible, be sure to upgrade the Windows Media Player to the latest version. ▥

Supported Video File Formats

When it comes to video, things get a bit tricky. The world of video formats is rapidly changing as companies keep trying to make smaller file sizes with better image quality. Additionally, the introduction of Digital Rights Management (DRM) has further complicated compatibility. Here's a list of file formats that will work natively with PowerPoint 2007. Again, the easiest solution is to stick with these formats whenever possible.

Windows Media file—Advanced Streaming Format (.asf)

This file format is designed to store synchronized multimedia data. It is used most commonly to stream audio and video content, images, and script commands over a network. In practical use, ASF is identical to WMV (described below), but starting with the Windows Media 9 Series, Microsoft uses only the WMV extension.

Windows Video file—Audio Video Interleave (.avi)

This is a common multimedia file format for storing sound and video. It is an older format that is also one of the most common. There are many different versions of AVI files because of several different audio and video codecs. These codecs are needed to decompress the video for playback on your machine. Do not assume compatibility; always test your AVI files before using them. If needed, the necessary codec can usually be found for free on the Internet.

MPEG Movie file—Moving Picture Experts Group (.mpg or .mpeg)

The MPEG format is an evolving set of standards for video and audio compression. It was developed by the Moving Picture Experts Group and was originally intended as a format for embedding video onto CD-ROMs and Video CDs. PowerPoint 2007 recognizes MPEG-1 files natively, but the newer MPEG-2 formats used by DVD and MPEG-4, formats which are commonly used on the Internet, are not compatible.

video.wmv

WMV file—Windows Media Video (.wmv)

These highly compressed files use a version of the Windows Media Video codec. The files are an efficiently compressed format that requires a minimal amount of storage space. Many Windows applications can create WMV files, and you can always download the free Windows Media Encoder from Microsoft's Web site (www.microsoft.com/downloads).

Why Won't a File Work?

While your sound or movie file may have the same file extension as one listed above, it still may not work. You need to make sure you have the correct version of the codec installed. Additionally, users of older operating systems can encounter compatibility issues with newer file formats. Try to keep your Windows Media Player up to date with the latest supported version for your Operating System. ▥

CAUTION

Broken Links Ahead. It is a very good idea to organize your media files. Create a folder for each presentation, then within that folder, add the following:

- the actual presentation file
- an audio folder
- a video folder
- an images folder
- a sources folder

Managing Your Media

While understanding how PowerPoint manages its relationships to media files is not a fun topic, it is an important one. You have two major options: to link to a file on your hard drive or to embed the file into your presentation. Knowing how both methods work will impact your workflow.

Embedding a Sound

Only .wav (waveform audio data) sound files can be embedded into a presentation. This means that the actual audio file is inserted into the file of the presentation and that the source audio is not needed.

By default, .wav sound files that are larger than 100 kilobytes (KB) are automatically linked to your presentation. If you want to embed them, you'll need to modify your Office options. Click the Office Button then choose PowerPoint Options. Select the Advanced category and adjust the Save options. You can choose to Link sounds with a file size greater than 50,000 KB. Raising this limit will increase the file size of a presentation, but can eliminate linking errors.

Linking a Sound or Video

When you insert a linked sound or video file, PowerPoint creates a link to the file's current location. If the file is moved, then the link breaks. It is a good idea to copy the sounds and videos into the same folder as your presentation before you insert them.

Package for CD

If planning in advance is not an option, then PowerPoint has a different strategy to help you. The Package for CD feature will copy all the files to one location (a CD or folder). Additionally, your presentation will automatically update the links for the new location of the media files.

To access this command in PowerPoint 2007 click the Office button then choose Publish > Package for CD. This is an important step if you plan to give the presentation using another computer or send it to another user. ▥

Inserting Audio on a Slide

Add Multiple Audio Files to a Slide and Establish Triggers to Play

1. Prepare Your Files

In order to complete this exercise (and others in this chapter) you'll need to copy the files to your computer. From the project CD-ROM, open the HTW Project Files folder and copy the Chapter 4 folder to your local hard drive. This folder contains all of the files needed for this chapter. Open the file Ch4_All_Star_Music_Starter.pptx and switch to slide 4.

2. Add Sound Files

When you want to add sound to a slide, first you need to select the slide. Click the Slides tab and select slide 4 **A**. In the Ribbon, click the Insert tab. From the Media Clips group, click the arrow under Sound. Choose the option Sound from File **B**.

Navigate to the Chapter 4 folder that you copied to your computer. Open the Audio folder and select the file 1 My Times.mp3. Double-click to insert the file.

3. Specify Playback

You must now specify how the file should play back. In the Microsoft Office PowerPoint dialog box you have two choices: a file can play back automatically when you get to the slide or play when it is clicked **A**.

Choose "When Clicked" to manually trigger the sound when you click its icon. A speaker icon appears on your slide and will act as a trigger. It is called a trigger because you must click the icon to activate the effect.

Drag the speaker icon and reposition it on the page. Place the speaker icon next to the type "My Times" **B**.

Repeat for the other two audio files.

4. Specify Playback Volume

By default, sound files will come in at Medium volume. You can modify this so the audio plays at a louder volume. This is important, as low volume level is a frequent complaint about presentations.

Click the first speaker icon, and then select the Options tab in the Ribbon **A**. Click the Slide Show Volume button and set the volume to High **B**. Repeat for the other two sound files.

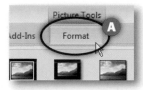

5. Clean Up Icons

Our final step may seem minor, but it's the details that truly polish a presentation. When you positioned the speaker icons, you did so visually. While this works, it is not the cleanest way to position items. PowerPoint offers an alignment command.

Select all three speaker icons by holding down the shift key and clicking on all three icons. Select the Format tab **A** from the Ribbon and click the Align button. Choose Align Objects Left to precisely align the speaker icons. Then choose Align > Distribute Vertically **B**.

The icons are now professionally aligned on the page. ▥

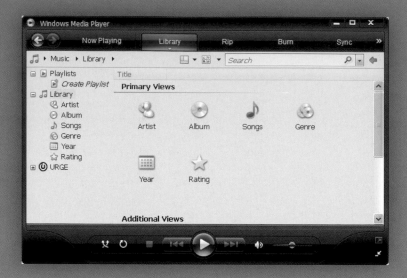

Extract Audio with Windows Media Player

Audio Can Be Extracted From a CD to a File for PowerPoint

1. Launch Windows Media Player

From the Start menu, launch Windows Media Player. This application should be installed by default on your computer. If not, you can download it from Microsoft's Web site for free.

2. Insert an Audio CD and Select Songs

Insert an audio CD into your computer's disc drive. If you are on the Internet, Windows Media Player will attempt to download information about the CD. Click the Rip tab to extract the files. By default, all tracks are selected to be copied (as long as you have not previously copied them from the CD). Clear the check box next to the track name if you do not want to import a track.

3. Specify Copy Settings

If you've never copied audio before, Windows Media Player will prompt you to choose settings on first import. If you've previously copied files, then click on the Rip tab and chose More Options to specify a format. The Windows Media Audio format works well, but be certain to uncheck the option to Copy Protect Music (otherwise you can run into issues when playing the audio on another computer).

T I P

Copy to Presentation Folder. You can select the needed audio files in your My Music folder and press Ctrl+C to copy them to your clipboard. Then navigate to your presentation folder and choose Ctrl+V to paste the files.

4. Copy Selected Tracks

Click the Start Rip. By default, the selected tracks are copied to your My Music folder. ▥

Extract Audio with Apple iTunes

Are You an iPod User? iTunes Works for PowerPoint

1. Launch iTunes

From the Start menu, launch Apple's iTunes. If you use an iPod, this is likely already installed on your system. If you don't have it, you can download from Apple's Web site for free (www.apple.com).

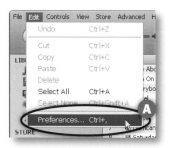
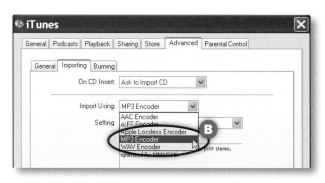

2. Set Your Import Preferences

You need to set your import settings to make them compatible with PowerPoint. From iTunes choose Edit > Preferences **A**. From the new window, click the Advanced tab then choose Importing. You can then choose to import with the MP3 or WAV encoder **B** for maximum compatibility with PowerPoint. Click OK to save the Importing preferences.

3. Insert an Audio CD and Select Songs

Insert an audio CD into your computer's disc drive. If you are on the Internet, iTunes will attempt to download information about the CD. By default, all tracks are selected to be copied. Deselect any songs you don't want to import by clearing the check box next to the track name.

T I P

Find an Audio File Quickly. You can select a track in your iTunes library and press Ctrl+R to reveal the file on your hard drive.

4. Import the Selected Tracks

Click the Import CD button. By default, the selected tracks are copied to My Music > iTunes > iTunes Music folder.

Insert Video on a Slide

Adding Video to a Slide Allows You to Create an Engaging Experience

Using Movies on Slides. In Power-Point 2007, you can use desktop video files with formats such as WMV, AVI, or MPEG. Additionally, you can insert an animated GIF file to display a graphic with animation. While GIFs are treated as movie clips, not all movie options are available for ani-mated GIF files.

Unlike pictures, movie files are always linked. This means that your PowerPoint file will look in the original location for the video file. It is a good idea to copy the video file into the project folder (see Caution: Broken links ahead).

1. Select the Slide to Add Video

This exercise uses the same presenta-tion file as the last exercise. If it's not already open, copy the Chapter 4 folder from the book's CD-ROM and open the Ch4_All_Star_Music_Starter.pptx and switch to slide 5.

2. Add a Movie to the Slide

On the Insert tab, in the Media Clips group, click the arrow under Movie. Choose the Movie from File option **A**. Navigate to Chapter 4 > Video folder and choose the file muse.wmv and click OK **B**.

3. Specify Playback

You must now specify how the video file should play back. In the Microsoft Office PowerPoint dialog box you have two choices: a file can play back automatically when you reach the slide, or manually when the preview icon is clicked.

Choose "When Clicked" to manually trigger the video when you click its thumbnail preview icon. A thumbnail preview is added to the slide and will act as a trigger.

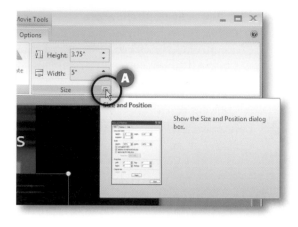

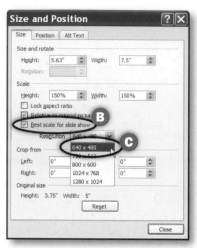

4. Size and Position the Movie

From the Options tab, locate the Size group. Click the small icon next to Size to show the Size and Position dialog box **A**. To avoid distortion, select the Lock aspect ratio option. In order to scale the movie larger with the best visual appearance, select the Best scale for slide show **B** and set the Resolution to 640 x 480 **C**. Click Close when finished with the sizing options. Reposition the movie to center it on the slide.

5. Specify Playback Volume

By default, video files will come in at Medium volume. You can modify this so the video plays at a louder volume. Be sure the movie file is selected, then click the Slide Show Volume button and set the volume to High. Double-click the movie's thumbnail icon to preview the clip.

6. Add the Second Movie

There's one more clip to add to the slide show. Below, we'll modify its settings to play back full screen. Switch to slide 6 and choose to Insert a movie file. Use the file yearforme.wmv, from the same folder as the previous clip. Choose to play the clip When Clicked and select OK.

7. Play a Movie Full Screen

You can set a movie so that it fills up the entire screen when you play it back. Be sure the recently added video clip is still selected and click the Options tab. From the Movie Options area, set the clip to Play Full Screen. This will launch the video full screen when clicked during a presentation.

8. Test the Movie

Now is a good time to check the slide show for playback. Select the Slide Show tab and click the From Current Slide (Shift + F5) button to preview the slide show. The presentation launches full screen. Click the movie's thumbnail to launch the movie full screen **A**.

The clip begins to play full screen **B**. To stop playback click the clip again. To exit full screen mode, press the Escape key. To exit the slide show press the Escape key once more.

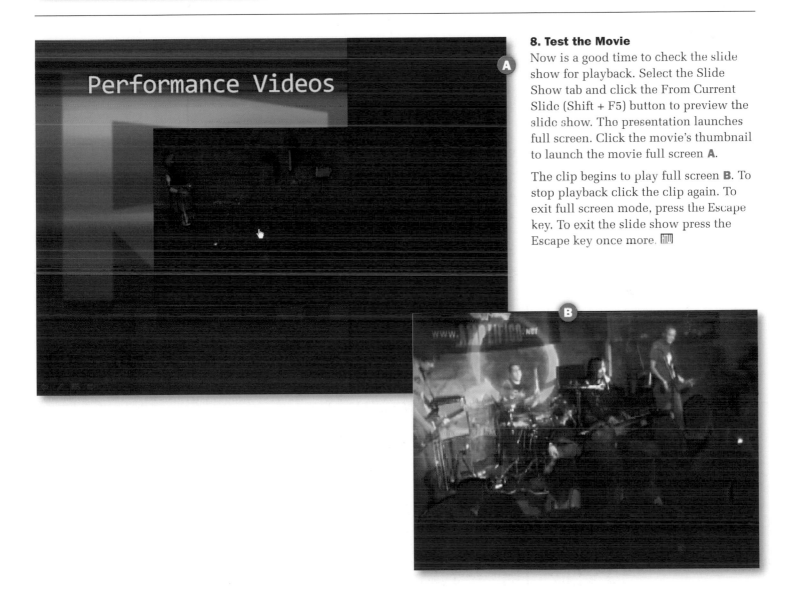

Putting Flash in a Presentation

Flash Significantly Extends the Animation Abilities of PowerPoint

---

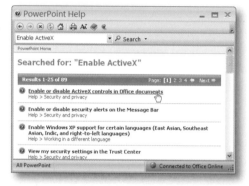

1. Enable Flash Technology

There are several preferences you must modify to enable Flash files. You may need to adjust your security settings to allow Active X to run (this is the portal for Flash). To activate ActiveX, go to the PowerPoint Help file and enter the text "Enable ActiveX."

Next, make sure that the Shockwave Flash plug-in has been loaded on your system. For maximum compatibility you should download the latest version from www.adobe.com. You should also install the latest version of Flash Player on your system.

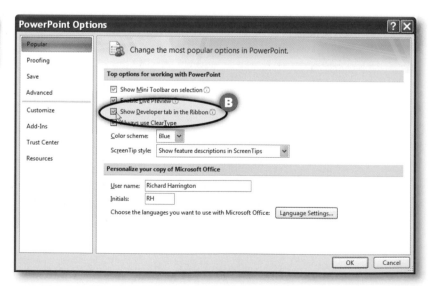

2. Enable the Developer's Tab

The Developer's tab contains several advanced elements that let you customize a presentation. Most of these are for developers, that is, those individuals who are actually using PowerPoint as a programming environment to create interactive programs.

To enable these tools, click the Microsoft Office Button **A**, and then click the PowerPoint Options button. Next, click Popular, and then under Top options for working with PowerPoint, select the Show Developer tab in the Ribbon check box **B**. To apply the change, click OK.

3. Add the Flash Control

Let's try adding a SWF animation to a slide. Switch to slide 7 in the All Star Music presentation. On the Developer tab, go to the Controls group, and click More Controls **A**. In the new dialog box, select Shockwave Flash Object from the list of controls **B** and click OK. Draw on the slide to insert the control. The animation you are going to insert is full-screen, so drag from the top corner to the bottom corner, covering the entire slide. A white box with an X should now cover the entire slide.

T I P

Find the Path. If you right-click on a file, you can choose to view its properties. One of those properties is location; you can highlight it and copy the text to your clipboard. This contains the full path (minus the filename).

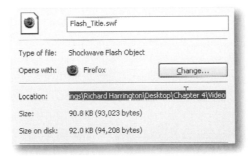

4. Locate the Movie

Unfortunately, the Flash control does not have a browse function to locate the movie. You have to know the actual file path (this is a long string of text such as C:\Documents and Settings\RHED Pixel \Desktop\Chapter 4\Sources\Video\ Flash_Title.swf). Be sure to figure out the location of your file. In the Chapter 4 folder you copied at the start of the lesson, open the Video folder; inside is a SWF animation called Flash_Title.swf.

C A U T I O N

Where's the Loop? If you want to loop a file, the original SWF file must be set to Loop. Otherwise, modifying the PowerPoint loop setting will have no effect.

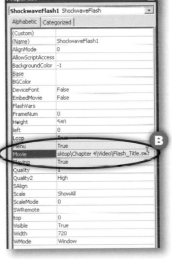

5. Modify the Control Container

Now that you know the location of the file, right-click the Shockwave Flash Object on the slide and choose Properties **A**. On the Alphabetic tab, click the Movie property (this specifies the file). In the value column (the blank cell next to Movie), type or paste the full drive path **B**, including the file name or URL to the Flash file that you want to play.

You can also set options such as looping by modifying settings in the Properties dialog box.

If you want to play the file automatically, set the Playing property to True. Another good idea is to set the file to embed into your presentation (this way you don't need to worry about links). Set the EmbedMovie property to True in order to automatically include the SWF animation inside the presentation **C**.

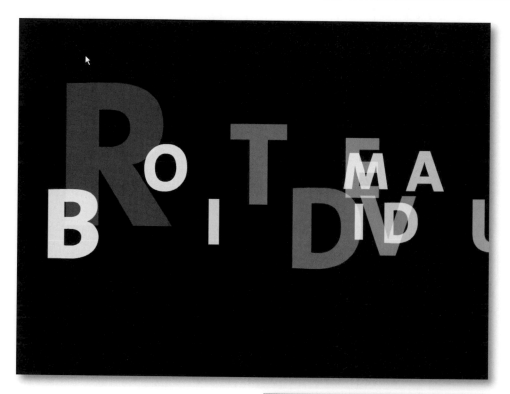

6. Test it Out

Lets see if it works. Press Shift+F5 to Preview the current slide. Did it work? Flash animations are a rapidly evolving feature inside of PowerPoint, so keep an eye on the built-in help menu to see if future updates streamline embedding a Flash file. If the above steps seem too in-depth, then be sure to check out PFCMedia, which shortens this process to a few clicks.

TIP

Rewind a SWF. If you successfully embed a Flash file, you'll soon discover that it's very difficult to rewind the Flash file to its beginning. To help with this, at http://skp.mvps.org/ flashback.htm you can download a free extension called FlashBack.

Unsupported Formats

There are a lot of competing media formats out there. There's a myriad of choices beyond Windows Media, and you'll likely encounter them when you're building a presentation, and many don't work with PowerPoint. Here are some types and suggested work-arounds if you need them.

QuickTime

QuickTime files are a common occurrence in both video and animation. Many creative software applications use QuickTime as an authoring format. However, Microsoft has virtually disabled all support for QuickTime files. For easiest integration, it is suggested that you convert your QuickTime files into a PowerPoint-compatible file.

- You can use QuickTime Pro ($29) to convert to an AVI file.

- You can install Flip4Mac to allow Mac users to create Windows Media files directly ($49–$179).

DVD Playback

There are a few approaches to using DVDs in a presentation. Such usage really comes down to what rights you have to the content and whether you'll have a DVD drive on the system you'll be presenting from.

- If a DVD drive is available, you can use PFC Media to embed a link to the actual DVD into your presentation (this is Microsoft's suggested workflow).

- If you have a non-copy-protected DVD, you can use DVD extraction software. A Web search will show you plenty of alternatives out there (our favorite is HandBrake).

> **CAUTION**
>
> **Don't Violate Copyright.** Just because you've purchased a DVD at the store does not give you the right to extract media from it. Additionally, the concept of "fair use" is often misunderstood and abused. If you are not an educator or a journalist, using a DVD for a commercial purpose (such as a sales presentation) can create legal issues. Needless to say, if it is a video created by your company, you most likely hold the rights. Be sure to visit www.copyright.gov for more information on usage rights.

Google Video

According to Google, there is no official support for PowerPoint on its system. But if you're patient, you can work around this block and still use many clips. With a little bit of conversion, you can create a compatible video. First, locate the video you want at http://video.google.com. Click the thumbnail to view the video. If there is a Download button, you can download an MPEG4 file by choosing Video iPod/Sony PSP from the menu and clicking Download.

After you've saved the video to your computer you will need to convert it to an AVI or WMV file. See the instructions above for converting QuickTime files and you'll soon have a video that's ready.

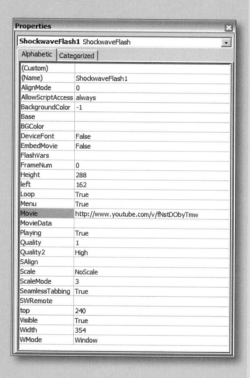

YouTube

If you're clever, you can get a YouTube video to work in PowerPoint. It's not easy, but it's pretty cool! The trick is to harness the power of Flash (see "Putting Flash in a Presentation"). The only difference is you'll insert a Web URL for the movie you want. For example if you found a movie like this: www.youtube.com/watch?v=973b_Dr8D5k you would view it on the page. What you need to do is modify the Web link. Instead, use www.youtube.com/v/973b_Dr8D5k to create a direct link to just the media file and none of the Web page navigation. When you launch your presentation, click once to start the clip. If you click the screen again it takes you to the YouTube Web site. Instead, click the space bar to advance the slide. 🖳

PlaysForCertain

Throughout this chapter we have brought you to a few stopping points you'll encounter when trying to embed media files into a PowerPoint presentation. There are certain features that Microsoft has chosen to leave out. Fortunately there's PlaysForCertain, two PowerPoint add-ins, that truly unlock multimedia power. These fill such a unique need that even Microsoft has chosen to suggest them in their help files (a search for inserting a DVD clip tells you to go and purchase these add-ins from PFCMedia).

There are two versions of the add-in PFC Media ($49) and PFCPro ($129). Both offer important features that harness the full abilities of Active X controls and Windows Media Encoder. In fact, Microsoft suggests you download and install the latest of both from its Web site—they're free). Let's take a look at the major features and how they can help you.

Media Management

When you insert a media file, PFCMedia automatically creates a copy and resolves linking issues. This is helpful as it saves you some extra work. Additionally, once the presentation is created, the playback machine does not need the specialty software loaded.

Play Commercial DVDs

PFC Media can actually play a DVD clip right inside of PowerPoint. The DVD must stay in your drive as it simply reads the file off the disc (extracting video clips from a DVD is generally seen as a violation of copyright). PFCPro gives you greater control and allows you to select clips from within PowerPoint and even specify exact start and end times. If you need the Closed Caption information from the DVD, then you'll also need the Pro version.

URL Linking for Media

Just enter a URL and the media is linked to and added to the presentation. This is good for items that need to frequently update. Speaking of URL linking, support for Webcams is also provided.

Formatting Options (Pro Only)

Just like with a photo, you can now discard extra pixels by cropping. You can also resize and recompress media to optimize it for disk space or smoother playback. Additionally, you can trim a clip to show only the portion you want.

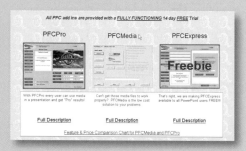

Worth Trying?

Fortunately, there is a fully functional 14-day trial, so if you have a multi-media heavy presentation coming up, download the software and give it a proper tryout. More details and the software can be found online at www.pfcmedia.com.

Adding Web Pages

Embedding a Web Page Lets You Bring Online Content Into a Presentation

1. Determine the Approach

Adding Web pages to a slide show is an essential task. There are two approaches to take. The path you choose will depend on whether or not you have an active Internet connection. Our first method is the method to choose if you are unsure about possible Internet connection options during your presentation.

2. Capture the Page

In case your Web connection goes down or is not available, it's a good idea to insert a static graphic of the Web page. You can do this by using the Print Screen command.

Launch a Web browser of choice such as Firefox or Internet Explorer. Visit the page for the band we've been profiling. Take your choice between www.myspace.com/amplifico or www.amplifico.net.

Press the Print Screen key on your keyboard to copy an image of the screen to your clipboard. Switch back to PowerPoint and go to slide 8 in the All Star Music presentation. Press Ctrl+V to paste the image into your slide.

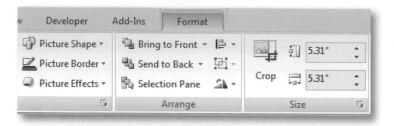

3. Format the Screen Capture

You can clean up the pasted image. With the image selected, click on the Format tab. You'll find numerous options to crop and clean up the image as well as stylize it with drop shadows or border effects.

4. Make the Link

With the image selected, right-click and choose Hyperlink **A**. The Insert Hyperlink dialog box opens. Add the Web page's address in the appropriately named Address field and click OK **B**.

5. Test the Link

You can press Shift+F5 to preview the presentation. To view the Web site, click on the screen capture and your Web browser will launch. To switch back to PowerPoint, press Alt+Tab to cycle applications (you may need to press the Tab key multiple times.) To exit the slide show when finished you can press the Escape key.

T I P

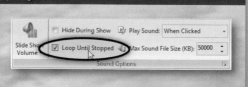

Loop a sound or movie to playback continuously. You can set a sound or movie to play back continuously on a single slide. Just click the sound or video icon to select it on the slide then click on the Options tab. Check the Loop Until Stopped check box. The sound (or movie) will keep playing until you advance to the next slide.

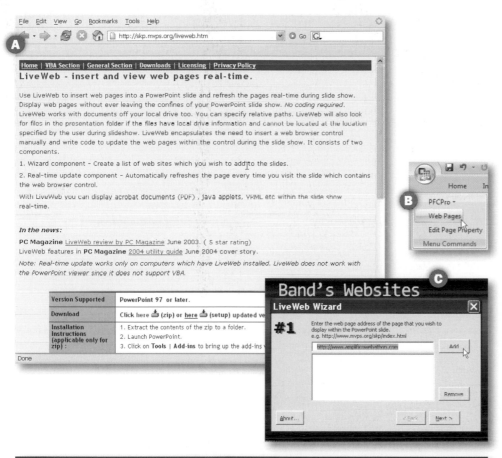

6. Another Way

If you are open to a free plug-in, you can download LiveWeb. This very useful add-on can be found at http://skp.mvps.org/liveweb.htm **A**. It allows you to embed multiple slides into a presentation using its wizard. Additionally, the Web pages are live via ActiveX and you can actually scroll through the page and click on live Web links. We usually chose to use both methods as a backup plan. Go ahead and insert a live Web page on page 9. After installing the free plug-in and relaunching, choose Add-Ins > Web Pages **B** and follow the LiveWeb wizard **C**. ▥

Play a sound or movie across multiple slides. You can set an audio or video file to play all the way through a presentation or a specific number of slides. Click the Sound or Video icon to select the file, then click the Animations tab. From the Animations group, click Custom Animation. In the Custom Animation pane, click the arrow to the right of the selected sound in the Custom Animation list, and then click Effect options. You can now modify the Stop Playing setting. Click "After," and then select the total number of slides on which the file should play.

CREATING CUSTOM THEMES & TEMPLATES

Take Ownership of Your Presentation's Design

THERE IS NOTHING MORE painful than seeing a presentation with the default PowerPoint background, the default type, and default colors accented with the preloaded Clip Art. Your organization may have a brilliantly designed graphic identity, but your presentation screams, "made by software out of the box." Almost all organizations and individual speakers use PowerPoint to deliver their message; now you can set yourself apart by taking advantage of the rich variations possible with custom themes and templates. Or you can use Adobe Photoshop to customize a background or image and make your presentation really stand out.

Themes

PowerPoint 2007's new Themes allows you to have 96,000 different combinations right out of the box. If you want to customize further, the possibilities are innumerable. If your presentation is set up correctly you can change the entire look of a presentation by just changing its Theme. It's fun to grab old presentations and apply some themes to them to see how they respond. In fact, if you have a library of presentations that are getting stale, you can open them up and apply your new, custom-branded theme to them. Making the change takes only a second, and it will appear that you worked around the clock as your organization's biggest brand cheerleader. After you've dusted off all of those old presentations, you'll be looking around for more things to add your magic touch to. Guess what? Themes also make it possible to create a cohesive look across an entire organization. You can apply your theme to Word, Excel, and Outlook files as well. They'll all have consistent fonts, colors, and styles.

Mastering Your Domain

Knowing how to build your presentation around Slide Masters will save you time, money, sleep, and sanity. The concept works hand in hand with Themes. You want to always be able to make global changes throughout your entire presentation in minutes, not hours. You may discover that when you get to the convention center to test your presentation, the smallest bullet point is too small to read from the back row. Or maybe there will be an issue with the level of contrast between your background and text. With properly set up Slide Masters, these problems and others can be solved across a massive presentation instantly.

Getting Creative

Putting together dynamic-looking presentations with relevant support graphics was infinitely more challenging 10 years ago. Now companies are scrambling for our attention to get us to use their images and templates. There are many ways to enhance your slides with imagery, and these methods get easier every day. Standard practice used to involve looking through printed stock-photo catalogs. After finding the right image, we'd call our rep to give her the resolution specs for the drum scanner and have the image rushed back to us by the end of the week to make our presentation deadline. Now, it's possible to create an online light box and review photo and illustration possibilities remotely with your client. You can get approval, download the images and have them in your presentation in minutes. With digital photography, you can shoot photos of a trade show floor and have them integrated into your slides just minutes later for a presentation.

Tyler Ryan Gel Mattress
CUSTOMER SERVICE

Modifying Existing Themes

By far the easiest and most efficient way to create a custom theme is to modify one that already exists. The development team at Microsoft invested quite a bit of research and development time in creating themes that work. They also listened to their customers and made sure that just about everything can be customized to create infinite new design possibilities. Building on something that already works is a great way to begin.

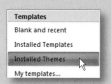

Where to Start

When you click the Office Button in PowerPoint and select the New button, you're given a series of choices. The best place to start is right in the Installed Themes section. All of these themes are fully customizable to meet just about any presentation need.

A Good Foundation

It's best to select a theme with a layout that is somewhat close to what you are looking for. It's simple to make a few subtle changes to a theme to create an entirely original look. The fewer changes that need to be made to achieve a unique look, the more efficient you'll be.

T I P

More Themes. Look at the Microsoft Office Online Web site at http://office. microsoft.com for more Themes. Check back every so often for updates.

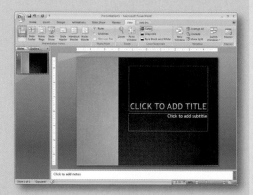

Where Are All My Slides?

When you create a new document based on Installed Themes, the document will open with just one slide thumbnail on the left of your main slide viewing pane. To get a better appreciation of all the layout possibilities in the theme, you'll need to view the Slide Master in the Presentation Views group under the View tab. All of the slides under the top Slide Master are called Layouts.

Slide Master

While still in Slide Master view **A**, you can experiment with global changes. If you make changes to the font on the Slide Master that include text effects, these changes are reflected in all of the subordinate layouts **B**. Bullet style changes made in the Slide Master will carry over to layouts within that theme as well. You can also make global changes to anchor graphics or backgrounds that appear on the Slide Master.

Rogue Slides

Sometimes you'll want a unique look for a layout that fits within the overall look of the theme but stands out from all of the other layouts. When you are modifying an existing theme, you can identify these layouts when you are making global changes. They will not comply. You can edit a single layout by double-clicking the thumbnail and making changes directly in the main viewing pane.

Colors

You'll notice that as you make modifications to existing themes, sometimes the colors will refuse to comply with your changes. This can mean that an integrated graphic element is not an editable shape or image with a recolor property applied. If you've selected a shocking purple theme because you liked the layout, you can instantly change the presentation's overall color scheme by selecting a color palette from another installed theme.

Fonts

PowerPoint has decided that it will allow only two fonts per theme. While this may seem restrictive, having only two fonts will help maintain consistency throughout your presentation. Keeping your presentation restricted to one Heading font and one Body font from slide to slide will ensure a professionally designed look. The place to start when modifying the fonts for your new theme is within the presets. Select the Slide Master and then open up the Fonts drop-down menu in the Edit Theme group and roll your cursor over the font sets in the Built-In group. As you roll over each set, you'll be able to see instant feedback on your slide.

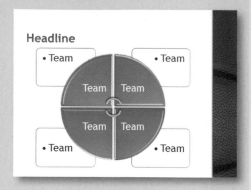

Effects

You'll have a variety of effects available to you that will use your theme colors. You can decide if you want your theme to have, among others, a flat vector-art look, a textured look, or a polished, metallic look with drop–shadows. The key with effects is to use them in moderation. Once you've decided upon a look for your theme, stick with it.

Saving Your Custom Theme

Once you're happy with your new theme, save it by clicking the Themes button in the Slide Master tab, and then selecting Save Current Theme in the drop-down menu **A**. Now when you browse through your theme thumbnails, your theme will be listed under the Custom group **B**.

Setting a Default Theme

If you know that you are building this theme as the cornerstone of many presentations that need to have a consistent look and feel, then it's a good idea to set it as your default theme. In the Design tab, right-click the thumbnail of the theme that you would like to make your default and then select the Set as Default Theme button. It's also a good idea to encourage anyone else who's responsible for presentation creation to do the same. It's easy to apply your custom theme after a presentation has been created, but having the right theme set as a default on the entire presentation team's computers will prevent inconsistencies. ▦

Building a Theme from Scratch

Designing Every Aspect of a Custom Theme

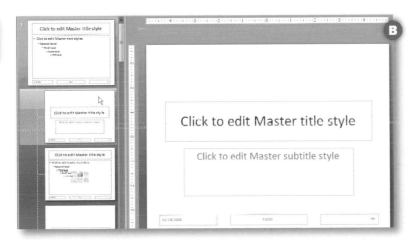

1. Start Fresh

From the project CD-ROM, open the HTW Project Files folder and copy the Chapter 5 folder to your local hard drive. This folder contains all of the files needed for the projects in this chapter. Click the Office Button and select New from the drop-down menu. Then select the Blank Presentation within the Blank and Recent group. A completely bare-bones slide opens up in your main viewing pane, with a placeholder for a title and subtitle. There is much more to this "blank" presentation than meets the eye. Under the View tab click the Slide Master button in the Presentation Views group **A**. Even though this is a blank presentation, PowerPoint is assuming that you'll probably need a few layouts to get started **B**.

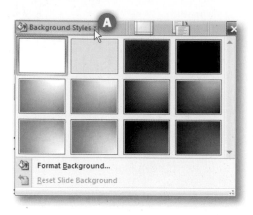

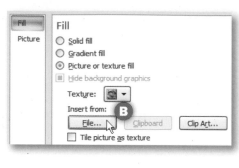

2. Background

Most of your layouts will depend upon the look of your background. Background design elements will dictate where text and images will be the most readable and pleasing to the eye. Your Theme colors will dictate the default backgrounds available in the Background Styles drop-down menu. While still in the Slide Master tab, click the Background Styles button in the Background group **A**. Then click the Format Background button to open up other options besides just gradients. Now click the Picture or texture fill radio button and then click the Insert from: File button **B**. Navigate to the images folder inside the Chapter 5 folder that you copied to your computer and select tan_waves.jpg.

3. Accent Bars

Now we'll go into our layouts and add in an accent bar. Click on the Title Slide Layout (the first layout under the Slide Master) **A**. Then click the Insert tab in your Ribbon and Select the Shapes button in the Illustrations group. Select the first rectangle in the Rectangles group **B**. Your cursor will turn into cross-hairs. Click and drag from the upper left corner of the layout until you have a solid masthead bar **C**. Repeat this step to form additional top horizontal bars and left vertical bars on various layouts in your theme.

4. Adjust Content Areas

The vertical blue side bar has carried over a graphic theme to the next slide, but now it has obstructed the Master title placeholder, as well as the content placeholder below it. Click each content window and then click on the handles on the left side and drag them to the right **A**. Now the content on your main title slide will no longer be obstructed. To make sure that you've aligned each content window accurately, select them both by holding down the shift key and clicking each one. Next, click the Format tab, and then click the Align Left button in the Align drop-down menu **B**.

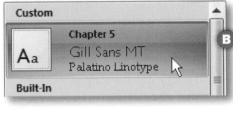

5. Fonts

In the Slide Master tab, select the Fonts drop-down menu in the Edit Theme group and then select the Create New Theme Fonts button **A**. Select any two fonts on your system and name your new Theme fonts "Chapter 5." Now when you select the Fonts drop-down menu in the Themes group, your new custom font theme is on top of the list **B**.

6. Theme Colors

To customize the colors, click the Colors drop-down menu in the Edit Theme group. Now select the Create New Theme Colors button **A**. The Create New Theme Colors window opens to reveal a series of variables for light and dark backgrounds. Theme colors are broken up into three categories—Text, Accent, and Hyperlink. Text colors are then subdivided into colors that show enough contrast on light backgrounds and colors that will stand out on dark backgrounds.

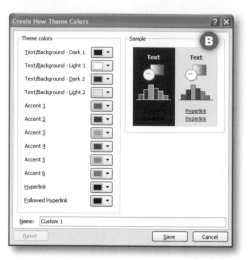

Accent colors and Hyperlink colors need to be visible on both light and dark backgrounds. In the Sample window with a light and dark background split screen, PowerPoint will show you if your colors are on target **B**. Select each color and modify it. In your sample window, review how much contrast the color has on both light and dark backgrounds. In the name field, type "Chapter 5" and click Save.

7. Save It

In your Slide Master tab click the Themes button in the Edit Themes group, then click the Save Current Theme button. In the File Name field type "Chapter 5" and click Save.

Slide Masters

The easiest way to have total control over a presentation is to have a good knowledge of its Slide Master and subordinate layouts. If you stay true to the Slide Master when populating your presentation, it won't be necessary to pull an all-nighter when last minute changes arrive. And they will—we promise.

What Is a Slide Master?

The Slide Master is where all of your globally editable information resides. Within the Slide Master are your backgrounds, font and bullet design choices, and content place holders. The Slide Master determines the font size, style, colors, and bullet treatment for the entire presentation.

Layouts

Each subordinate layout begins its life as a copy of the Slide Master. Content areas are added to give each layout a more specific purpose. Think of your favorite magazine. There are specific ways a feature story is handled. There is a specific way the table of contents page and the letters to editor page are laid out. These layout styles give the reader a sense of consistency throughout the publication even though each one has unique attributes. PowerPoint uses the term layout in the same fashion.

Placeholders

Each layout contains a placeholder for content. When designing layouts in the Slide Master view, you must use the Insert Placeholder command if you want to be able to edit that content in the Normal View. Placeholders are designed to position text and objects like graphics, charts, tables, and media neatly on a slide. They make it clear where you need to add specific content when building a presentation.

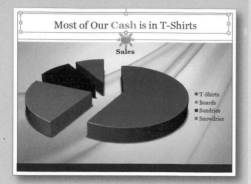

What Can Be Modified in the Normal View?

You can modify fonts and placeholder positions in the Normal View. You can also modify an individual slide's background. A layout is a suggestion; some rules are made to be broken. You may discover that a layout usually works well, but for one specific slide the content area is not large enough to accommodate a chart or text. Content areas or place-holders can be resized in the Normal View if needed. It's also possible to change a font or font characteristics on just one slide for emphasis.

Multiple Masters

It's possible to have multiple masters in one presentation. To demonstrate why this is important, we had some fun with a fictional Sun & Snow presentation. There is a consis-tent brand throughout all the slides; however, within individual slides there is a distinct look for the summer season and one for the winter season. With two complete sets of Slide Masters and Layouts, it's possible to do a yearly overview in one presentation incor-porating both Masters. It's also possible to focus on just one master if necessary.

Making Global Changes

Proper preparation gives you the ability to make global changes instantly. If your boss tells you that she prefers a stronger, heavier font on all of the titles, you can make one change to the Slide Master and Layouts and it's immediately reflected on all of your slides. Can you imagine if you needed to reposition a logo that you'd copied and pasted on each slide of an 80-slide presentation? It would take quite a bit of time. If the logo were positioned on a Slide Master Layout, you would only have to reposition it once and the change would be reflected on all 80 slides. It may seem easier to just make a little tweak here and there on a slide in Normal View, but it pays off in the long run to manipu-late everything with your Slide Master.

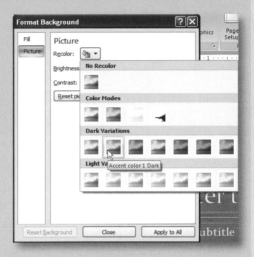

Building Masters for Flexibility

If you want to build a Slide Master that can reflect global changes in color, you'll need to make sure all of the images you've imported (including background images) are formatted with the Recolor option. For background images select the Format Background button under the Background Styles drop-down menu. Then select the Recolor button in the Picture group. Select a color from the Light or Dark Variations thumbnails. Next, select any other non-background photo and click Recolor under the Format tab in the Adjust group. Select a color from the Light or Dark Variations thumbnails. Using that option assigns one of the six accent colors in a Light or Dark Variation to colorize the image. If the Theme colors are changed, your image will reflect those changes. Keep in mind however that this will dramatically affect how your color images look. If you need to maintain the image's original look, then it will not be an option to reflect global changes in color by changing the Theme colors.

Setting Animations Globally

You can assign animations to your Slide Master Layouts. Assigning animations in this manner will allow you to maintain consistency and to have the option to change your animations globally. We can assure you that no matter how you set up your animations, someone will suggest changing them. They'll be either too fast or too slow, or too distracting, or not exciting enough. If they're all set up in the Master Layouts, your response will be, "No problem." It's also useful to be able to change the presentation's timings globally to advance some slides automatically and have others driven by the presenter. We will cover animation in Chapter 6. ▥

Finding Source Material

Building custom templates requires source images. You'll need textures and photos to create your own backgrounds. By using your own images, you can craft the perfect look to carry your message. We've personally witnessed a day of presentations where the same three templates kept popping up. It's important that your messages come wrapped in their own look, otherwise they will just blend into all the rest and become digital noise.

Microsoft Office Online

One of your first stops should be Microsoft Office Online. You can browse for artwork in the Clip Art task pane inside PowerPoint. From the task pane you can click the Clip Art on Office Online button to launch a Web browser and search through more than 150,000 pieces of artwork and sound effects. These images are all cleared for you to use in presentations. The primary advantage of this system is that you can browse the files and add them to your basket. When you are done shopping, you just go to "checkout" and the images are downloaded (for free) into the Microsoft Clip Organizer.

Stock Photo Web Sites

The stock photography industry is a source of great creativity. There are thousands of providers who offer a myriad of choices and licensing options. Some of the highest profile Web sites can be very expensive, but don't get turned off. Those higher fees are often for exclusive licenses or to cover model and photographer fees. With a little bit of searching you'll be able to find high-quality images that match your budget. Here are a few of our personal favorites:

- *www.iStockphoto.com*—Most images cost between $1.00 and $10.00, with several options to choose from. This site is constantly updated with new options and is easy to search.

- *www.Shutterstock.com*—This Web site offers a variety of subscription plans. It has a large collection, but limits you to 25 downloads a day.

- *www.Clipart.com*—This extensive Web site boasts over 6 million downloads. The site offers short-term membership plans from one week, but greater savings are with monthly and annual plans.

- *www.Fotolia.com*—This Web site offers several options and search criteria. Images are affordably priced at $1.00 to $3.00 per image.

- *www.Stockxpert.com*—This extensive Web site features great organization and images. Most low-resolution images are priced at $1.00 to $2.00.

T I P

Getting the Resolution Right.
Most stock images Web sites offer photos at various resolutions. The size you needs will depend on output. Usually the more expensive images are intended for high-resolution print output. You'll usually be able to get away with the lower quality or multi-media files. Just look at an image's sizing details (measured in pixels). Generally, if an image is 1024 x 768 pixels (or greater), it will work in your presentation.

Free Image Web Sites

You need to be careful when browsing "free" image Web sites. There are a lot of images viewable online, but that does not mean they are free to use. For example, nearly every image you'll find using Google Image Search (www.images.google.com) is copyrighted. Be sure to look for usage rights and explicit permission to use images you find online. If you're careless you can open yourself up to major legal and financial risk. Here are some free image sites or directories worth checking out:

- *Raster/Vector Free Images page* (www.rastervector.com/resources/free/free. html)—This is a blog and resource site on computer graphics that we run. On this page you will find links to numerous government Web sites with high-quality images that are made available for free (specific usage rights on each Web site).

- *Morgue File* (www.morguefile.com)—This Web site provides a large variety of images that are generally free to use (see its Terms page).

- *Flickr's Creative Commons pool* (www.flickr.com/creativecommons)—This directory site allows you to search through images that others are sharing for use with Creative Commons licenses.

- *Everystockphoto* (www.everystockphoto.com)—This Web site also indexes items that are made available through Creative Commons licenses.

Digital Camera

Even if you don't consider yourself a good photographer, a digital camera can come in handy to take photos of what you need. You can spread objects out on a conference table and start shooting your own backgrounds. Take a quick field trip, and you'll come across all sorts of great textures that you can use to start your own backgrounds. To inspire and motivate you, we've included some digital photos that we've taken. You'll find them on the book's CD-ROM in the Stock Photos folder.

From Your Organization

If you are creating a template for your office, association, or professional group, chances are it already has some print materials or a Web site. Find out what assets already exist. Are there photos and a color palette? Perhaps someone has already purchased stock images and locked in a "look." If you are creating a new presentation template, always check first to see if any assets exist. 📖

Creating Custom Backgrounds in PowerPoint

Photoshop-Style Techniques for PowerPoint

1. Open a Blank Presentation

Let's start with a Blank Presentation. Click the Office Button and then select the New button. Click the Blank and recent button. Once you've created a background that you're happy with, we'll show you how to convert it for use in any later presentation.

2. Add the Background on the Master

If you create the background on the Slide Master, it will automatically populate all of the slides in your template. Open the View tab and select the Slide Master button in the Presentation Views group. Select the Slide Master. It's the first slide in the series of thumbnails on the left. In the Background group, click the Background Styles drop-down menu and then select Format Background. Select the Picture or texture fill radio button and then select the Insert from: File button. Navigate to the Images folder in the Chapter 5 folder that you previously copied to your computer and select tan_waves.jpg. Then click the Close button in the Format Background window.

3. Use a Shape to Carry a Photo

Now we'll add a photo on top of our background. To have a little more control of your image, place it within a shape. Click the Insert tab and select Shapes from the Illustrations group. Select the Round Single Corner Rectangle **A**. Your cursor will change into crosshairs. Click and drag to form a large shape on your screen. Now select the Format tab. Click the Shape fill button in the Shape Styles group and select Picture from the drop-down menu. Navigate to your Chapter 5 Images folder and select FatherandSon.jpg and this will fill your shape **B**.

4. Arrange the Photo

Scale the photo down by clicking on a corner handle and dragging toward the center of the photo **A**. Now position the photo so that the back edge of the toddler's head is aligned with the left edge of the slide **B**. In the Format tab select the No Outline button from the Shape Outline drop-down menu.

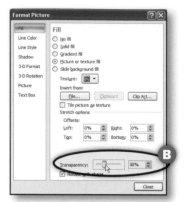

5. Composite the Photo with the Background

With the photo still selected, click the Shape Effects button in the Shape Styles group. Select 50 Point from the Soft Edges drop-down menu **A**. Now select the Format tab under Picture tools heading. In the Adjust group, click the Brightness button and select Picture Corrections Options. Now click the Fill button and adjust the Transparency to 30% **B**.

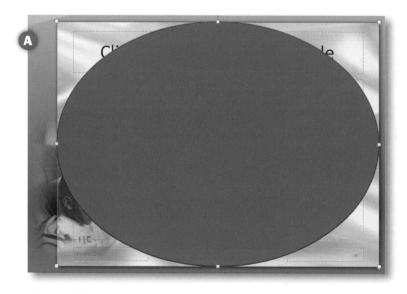

6. Add Another Photo

In the Insert tab select an oval and drag it so that it touches each edge of the slide **A**. In the Format tab select the Shape Fill drop-down menu and select Picture. Navigate to your Chapter 5 Images folder and select Boys.tif. Under the Picture Tools heading, select the Format tab. Click the Send to Back button in the Arrange group **B**.

7. Composite Photo

With your photo selected, click the Picture Effects button and select 50 point from the Soft Edges drop-down menu. In the Adjust group select the Recolor drop-down menu. Then select Accent Color 6, the last option in the Light Variations group. Now, in the Brightness drop-down menu in the Adjust group click on the Picture Corrections Options group. Click the Fill button and adjust the transparency to 50 percent.

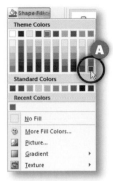

8. Blend It All Together

In the Insert tab, select a rectangle shape from the Shapes drop-down menu. Click and drag it so that it covers the entire slide. Select the Format tab and then click the Shape Fill drop-down menu. Select a warm brown color **A**. Now click the very well-hidden Format Shape button **B**. Click the Fill button and adjust the transparency to around 65 percent. Next, click the Shape Outline button and select No Outline from the drop-down menu to remove any unwanted color. The warm brown color overlay will help tie all of the colors together for a more cohesive look **C**.

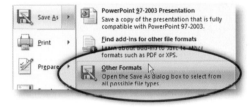

9. Convert the Composite into a Flattened Image

To improve your presentation's performance, it's best to convert this composited background into a flattened image. In the View tab select Normal in the Presentation Views group. In the Home tab select the New Slide button and select the Blank layout thumbnail. Click the Office Button and select Save As, and then select Other Formats. In the Save As type field, select JPEG. Next, in the pop-up window select Current Slide Only. ▥

Creating Custom Backgrounds with Photoshop Elements

This Feature-Rich Application Makes Backgrounds Easy

1. Download and Install the Free Trial

Adobe Photoshop is the number one computer graphics tool on the planet. It is used in nearly every industry, from Web design and magazine publishing to medical imaging and forensic science. But all that power can cost you. Fortunately Adobe has distilled some of that power into an affordable package that is well-suited for the business professional. Adobe Photoshop Elements is priced at only $89 to download or $99 in stores. For this you get to explore many options for creating backgrounds to use in PowerPoint. Download the free trial from Adobe's Web site (it will work for 30 days) in order to complete these exercises—www.adobe.com/products/photoshopelwin.

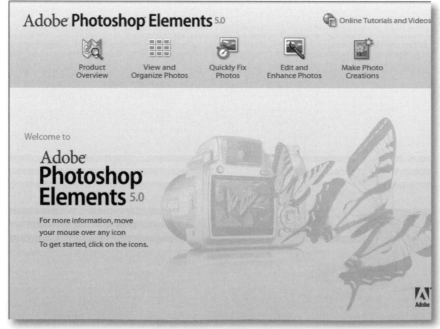

2. Launch Photoshop Elements

Download and install the Photoshop Elements trial. After installation is completed, launch the application. The Photoshop Elements welcome screen opens with choices for starting points. Click the Edit and Enhance Photos button to access complete controls. The application launches and presents you with an activation box. Click the Continue Trial button to continue using the program.

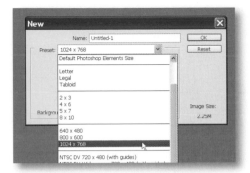

3. Create a New Document

Photoshop Elements can create a new document using predefined sizes. Choose File > New > Blank File to open the Document Window. Click the preset list and choose 1024 X 768 to create a document sized for a standard Power-Point presentation. Click OK to make the new document.

4. Create a New Background with Built-In Templates

There are several built-in templates for backgrounds that are included with Photoshop Elements. Select the Artwork and Effects window (if its not visible choose Window > Artwork and Effects). Click the category button to access built-in presets **A**. From the Category list choose Backgrounds **B**. Then from the subcategory list explore the different options **C**. For this exercise, choose the Nature subcategory and choose the Water Drop background. Double-click the thumbnail to apply the background.

5. Convert the Background into a Layer

Photoshop uses a system of overlapping artwork called layers. Each layer can hold artwork, text, or logos. In order to further modify the Background it needs to be converted into a layer. In the Layers palette, double-click in the word "Background." A new window opens asking you to name the layer. Call this layer Water Drops and click OK. Save your file by choosing File > Save. Name the file WaterBG.psd and click OK.

6. Get a Global View

For these next steps, it will be easier of you can see a global view of your image. In the upper-right-hand corner of the application window, click the Maximize Mode button **A** to bring the image window full-screen. In order to see the borders of your image, Choose View > Zoom Out until you can see a gray border around it **B**.

7. Add Screen Layers

In order to create backgrounds, we can screen back portions of the photo to make it lighter. These "empty" areas are well suited to hold text or charts. These screen layers will be created using a special adjustment layer. Select the Marquee tool by pressing the letter M, or click the Marquee in the Tools window **A**. Click in the top right corner and drag down to the left in the window to create a marquee selection that leaves a small strip of color on the left edge **B**. This selection will become the screened area. In the Layers palette, click the Adjustment Layer icon **C** and choose Hue/Saturation **D**.

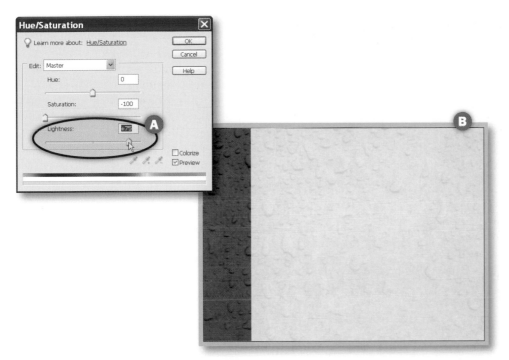

8. Adjust Saturation and Lightness

A new window opens that allows you to adjust the hue, saturation, and lightness of the selected area. Pull the Saturation slider to the left to desaturate the image (this removes all color). Next adjust the Lightness slider by dragging it toward the right **A**. Pick a value that creates a white textured background **B**.

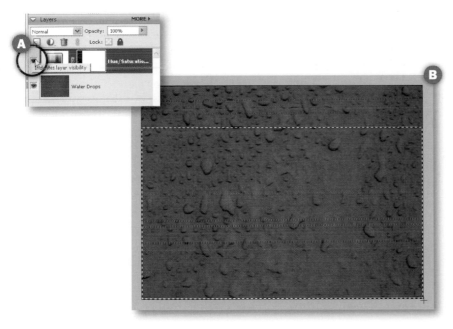

9. Make Another Background

Turn the adjustment layer off by clicking the eye icon next to its name **A**. You can now create a new selection using the Marquee tool. Create a rectangle selection that leaves a strip of color across the top edge **B**. Add a new Hue/Saturation Adjustment layer and adjust Saturation and Lightness to taste.

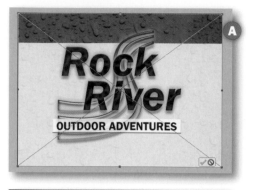

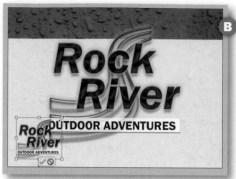

TIP

Logos with Transparency. If you need a logo with a transparent background, look for files with these extensions: .png, .eps, or .ai.

10. Add a Logo

One advantage to using Photoshop is that you can add a logo file to your slides and have it stay in a consistent position throughout your slide show. Choose File > Place and navigate to the chapter exercise folder you copied to your computer at the start of this lesson. Choose the file RockRiver.png and click Place. The logo is added to the center of your slide. Click Enter to apply the logo (this large version will serve as a title graphic) **A**. To make a smaller version, right-click on the logo in the Layers palette and choose Duplicate Layer. Name the layer RockRiver Small. Click on the corner of the logo and scale it down. Size the logo small and position it in the lower left corner **B**. Press Enter to apply the changes to the logo.

11. Save Your Work and Background Images

Before moving forward, it is a good idea to save your work. Press Ctrl+S to save your file. Your document has five layers and several combinations that will be useful for the PowerPoint template. By turning the visibility (eye) icons off and on for different combinations, you can create several different looks. Use the layer combinations shown here to create different options for PowerPoint **A**. After creating a combination, choose File > Save for Web. In the preset pick JPEG High **B** and click OK. In the file services box, pick a destination, give the file a unique name, and click Save.

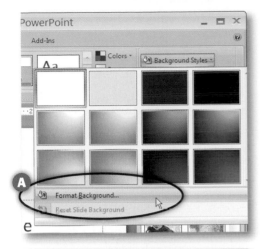

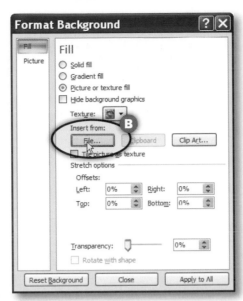

12. Close Photoshop and Switch to PowerPoint

Now that your images are saved as JPEG files, you can close Photoshop (be sure you've saved your work). You can now switch to PowerPoint and use these new background images in an existing Template or Theme (or create a new one). To add a background image, switch to the Design tab. In the Background group click the Background Styles button and choose Format Background **A**. In the Format Background window choose Picture or texture Fill, then click the File button **B** and navigate to the new background image and click Insert. When satisfied, close the window. 🖾

T I P

Create Even More. Now that you have a template built, creating new backgrounds is a snap. Just replace the logo layer with your own content. Additionally, you can easily swap out the WaterDrop layer and use additional textures found in Photoshop Elements, those included on the CD-ROM, or any of your own.

Creating a Custom Template

Often, you will need to create multiple presentations that cover the same type of information in a similar order. Once you have determined the best approach to guide your audience effectively through a presentation, it's a good idea to capture it and create a template that you can continue to refine as you receive feedback.

Themes

Where to Start

You can create a custom template from any presentation, or you can build one based on an existing theme. To illustrate the components of a template, we'll look at one that starts with a blank slate. Open up a new Blank Presentation. First, you should apply a Theme. You can find Themes under the Design tab. Earlier in the chapter we created a Theme called Chapter 5. Click the Chapter 5 thumbnail in the Themes group.

TIP

More Templates. Have a look at the Microsoft Office Online Web site (http://office.microsoft.com) for more templates. Keep in mind that you can download any template and update it using your preferred theme.

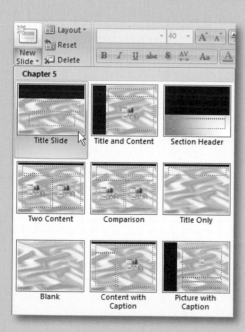

Layouts

Most Themes have a series of layouts built in for you to choose from. It's usually not necessary to incorporate every layout into a template. Decide which layouts will best suit your presentation and integrate them by clicking the New Slide button in the Home tab. When you click the New Slide button, the drop-down window will show you all of the available layouts in the Theme that you've selected.

Modifying Layouts

You may have different topics that you intend to cover such as divisions of a company, age groups in a study, or stages of a project. You can help your audience differentiate between topics by modifying the backgrounds, photos or accent colors of a particular layout in the Slide Master view. Click the Home tab. Select the slides that you would like to modify and then click the Duplicate Selected Slides under the New Slide button. Now you can select the items that you want to modify such as photos, font colors, object colors, and backgrounds in the Slide Master tab **A**. Be sure to rename each layout specifically using the Rename button in the Edit Master group **B**.

Corporate Logos

It's always best to start with a vector-based logo, as we discussed in Chapter 3. More often than not, however, you'll be faced with incorporating a raster-based logo into your template. You can import the logo as a picture and then manipulate it to integrate into the presentation. The logo will usually be rectangular in shape on import **A**. In the Picture Styles group under the Format tab **B**, you can manipulate the shape, border, and overall effects to match your presentation. Now the logo matches the presentation and is more dynamic and appealing **C**. Once the logo has been imported and modified, it can be copied, pasted, and resized to fit on any other Master Layout or individual slide.

> **INSIGHT**
>
> **Scaling 3-D Objects.** When you scale some 3-D objects, the Bevel, Depth, and Contour may need to be adjusted to conform to the new size.

Slide Content

When you incorporate new slides into your template, they are just physical representations of your Master Layouts. They will contain placeholder areas for text, charts, objects, and images. They will not provide an order or information for presentation organization. If you want guide your template user, type in sample text that is intended to go with the layout. This will help the template user understand how to best use each layout and help preserve consistency.

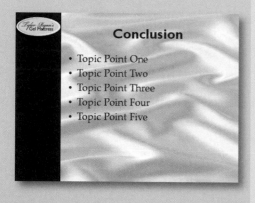

Refining the Template

When all your layouts have been modified, build a sample presentation. Order your slides logically. In our example we've put together a template that covers an executive overview. We've split up the company by division. Each division has a unique Section Header and is named appropriately. Here is your opportunity to make some suggestions. We've added a slide after our introductory slide that is titled "Presentation Goals," and we've also added a slide at the end titled "Conclusion." Each slide consists of a short series of bullets. This can work as a subtle reminder for the presenter to recap at the end of a presentation to aid in audience information retention.

Checking for Consistency

After proofing each slide of your template, it's often a good idea to view the entire template in Slide Sorter view. At a glance you can see if your template has a consistent look and if there are any glaring errors. This is also a good way to reorder your slides if the need for a better sequence becomes evident.

Saving Your Template

What makes a PowerPoint presentation a PowerPoint template is simply how you save it. Under the Office Button click Save As and then Click PowerPoint Presentation. In the Save as type: window be sure to select PowerPoint Template (*.potx) **A**. When you open a new presentation, by selecting the My Templates button you will have the option to select from all of the templates that you've created. Clicking this button will reveal a New Presentation window. Now you can review your templates by seeing each first slide in a Preview window and selecting the one you want **B**. ▥

6

ADDING MOTION & CREATIVE TRANSITIONS

Using Movement Within and Between Slides

OVERVIEW OF CUSTOM ANIMATION *102*

ANIMATING BULLETS *104*

ANIMATING A CHART *107*

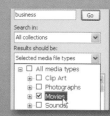

USING GIF FILES *110*

ANIMATING SMARTART *111*

THE THEORY OF TRANSITIONS *113*

ADDING TRANSITIONS TO SLIDES *115*

USING THIRD PARTY TRANSITIONS *117*

PROPER USE OF ANIMATION can enhance a presentation, while improper use can distract or even annoy your audience. So where does the dividing line lie between tasteful and tacky? That is often a judgment call that presenters must make based on their subject material and the makeup of their audience. Our personal tastes lean toward conservative, as we favor clean and elegant over flashy and over-the-top.

Good Animation Versus Bad Animation

Animation can reveal elements in a chart that help the presenter focus the audience's attention. Also through animation, multiple bullets on the same slide can be revealed one at a time in order to keep the audience from reading ahead. But when animation is no longer used for a purpose, but rather as an effect, it loses its proper impact. Sound effects and whiz-bang transitions are often overused. It is crucial that animation be properly balanced, or your presentation will suffer.

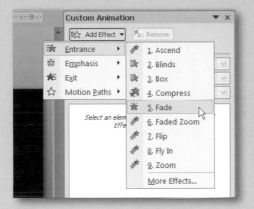

Animation on Slides

PowerPoint supports several different styles of animation. You can use Custom Animation Effects such as lines of texts or pieces of SmartArt to make elements enter your slide. Additionally, you can add emphasis to elements and have them grow, flash, and even flicker to draw a viewer's eye. When elements in a slide are done, they can then exit a slide to make room for more. And if the more than 100 preset animations don't work for you, animations can be customized using Motion Paths.

Animation Between Slides

Many presenters use a transition between each slide. These effects are similar to the many wipes used in film or television. A transition between slides can fade or wipe as well as push one slide out of the way to make room for another. In the strict language of cinema, a transition is only meant to signify a transition in time or location. In a presentation, this equates to changes in thoughts. For example, you might use no transition between multiple pages of text on the same topic, then a gentle transition like a fade to go to a new topic. Then, as you make the transition to a new section of the presentation, a more dramatic wipe could be used.

When to Use Motion

Motion can be effectively used to draw attention to a slide and to changes in thought. Well-placed motion can be the gentle nudge to refocus the audience's attention. But restraint is still a good idea. Watch any Academy–Award winning film and count just how many transitions are used. (We're often able to use just one hand.)

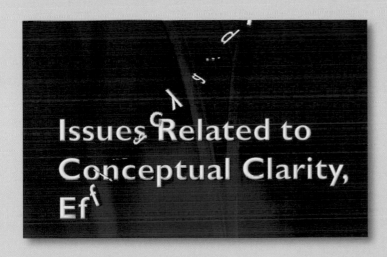

Overview of Custom Animation

The Custom Animation window offers several options to add animation within a slide. Click the Animations tab to access additional controls and then click the Custom Animation button. The Custom Animation task pane opens and unlocks four major categories of effects. These effects can be applied to any selectable element on a slide.

Entrance

The many Entrance effects can be used to add elements to a slide. PowerPoint organizes these effects into four subcategories: Basic, which offers a set of effects that use simple motion; Subtle, which uses gentle motion that is not distracting; Moderate, which uses more motion to draw attention to an element; and Exciting, which relies on large dramatic movements. The effect you choose should match the feeling you are trying to evoke. Are you gently switching from one topic to the next or do you really need to yell something aloud?

Emphasis

Emphasis effects can be added to elements on a slide that you'd like to draw attention to. These effects should be used sparingly, as they can be very distracting. The effects are grouped into the same four groups as the Entrance effects (Basic, Subtle, Moderate, and Exciting). These classifications can seem arbitrary, so you will want to test each effect before running your slide show.

Exit

Exit effects are the direct opposite of entrance effects. They can be used to remove objects from a slide to make room for new elements. Additionally, a negative build can be used to remove elements from a slide to create a topic of focus. The adding of exit effects is often overlooked, but they can be helpful when properly used. Exit effects are best used when you have several slides in a row with identical backgrounds. Instead of using transitions between slides, exit and entrance effects can be paired so one element flies out as another flies in.

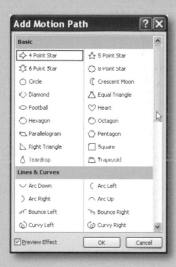

Motion Paths

Motion paths allow you to animate elements along straight or curved lines. These lines (or paths) can be used for both entrance and exit effects. PowerPoint offers 64 preset paths, organized into three categories: Basic, which uses several standard shapes such as stars, triangles, and others; Lines & Curves, which uses arcs and curves as well as angled lines to guide the animation; and the final category, Special, which uses more elaborate shapes as the motion path. Additionally, PowerPoint gives you the option to draw a Custom Path that best suits your needs.

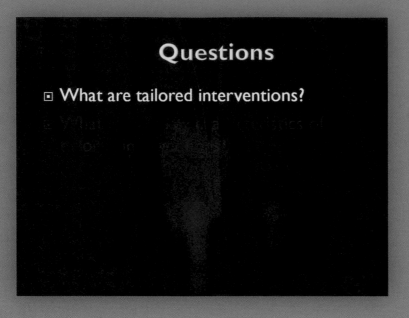

Animating Bullets

Creating Animated Text Can Add Emphasis to a Presentation

1. Open a Presentation

In order to complete this exercise (and others in this chapter) you'll need to copy the files to your local computer. From the project CD-ROM, open the HTW Project Files folder and copy the Chapter 6 folder to your local hard drive. This folder contains all of the files needed for this chapter. Open the file Ch6_Nursing.pptx.

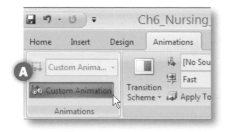

2. Access the Entrance Effects

In order to animate a block of text you need to select it. Switch to slide 9 in the Slides list and click the text block with three bullets. Click the Animations tab in the Ribbon and then click the Custom Animation button to open the Custom Animation task pane **A**. Click the Add Effect button and choose Entrance > More Effects **B**, and the Add Entrance Effect window opens.

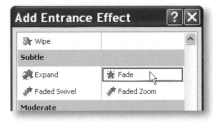

3. Animate the Text Entrance

The Add Entrance Effect window opens so you can browse different entrance effects. Make sure that the Preview Effect box is checked so you can see the effects without applying them. Scroll through the list and preview different effects by single-clicking them. After previewing multiple effects, choose Fade and click OK.

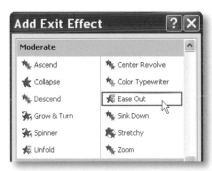

4. Animate the Text Exit

In addition to animating the entrance of the text you can animate the text's exiting the slide. In the Custom Animation task pane choose Add Effect > Exit > More Effects. In the Add Exit Effect window you can preview different effects by single-clicking on them. After previewing multiple effects, choose Ease Out and click OK. The effect is applied to each stage of the builds; however this is not desired, as it will slow down the transition to the next slide. Step 5, provides the solution to this problem.

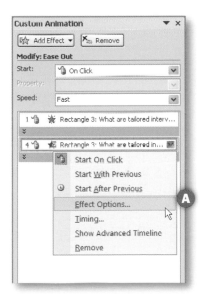

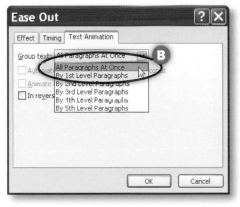

5. Modify the Exit Effect

In the Custom Animation pane, click the Exit effect. Click the drop-down menu on the right of the effect name and choose Effect Options **A**. A window opens with the name of the effect in its title bar. Click the Text Animation tab and switch Group text to All Paragraphs At Once **B**. Click OK to apply the change then the Play button to preview the effect.

6. Preview, Then Repeat the Effect

To see the effects on the slide, click the Play button at the bottom of the Custom Animation task pane. After previewing the effect, repeat it on the next slide. Select slide 10, then repeat the Entrance and Exit effects. If you'd like extra practice, you can animate the bullets on slides 6, 14, 15, 17, and 18.

7. Preview the Presentation

To understand how animation works, preview your work so far. Click on slide 9 in the Slides list. Choose Slide Show from the Ribbon. Click the button From Current Slide to preview the slide show. Click the space bar to advance the presentation. Each click will bring up one stage of the build. After the last bullet exits from the first slide, you will need to click again to start the next build. ▦

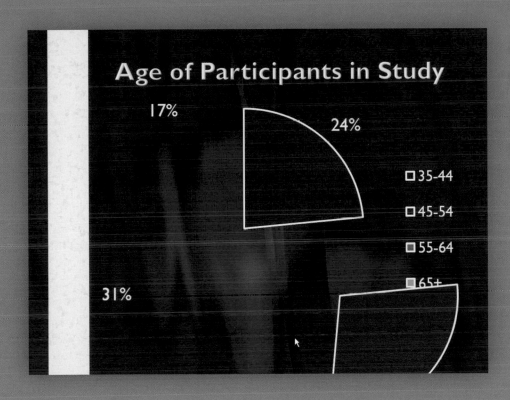

Animating a Chart

The Entrance of a Chart Can Be Animated

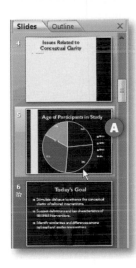

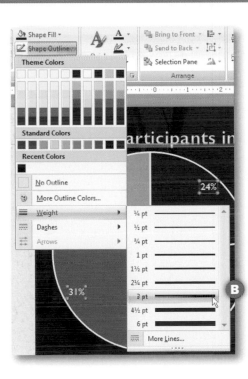

1. Prep the Chart—Lines

Before animating a chart, you should examine it to ensure it is ready for animation. Very thin lines and small text can be problematic, as they will shimmer when animating. Switch to slide 5 in the Slides list **A** and click the pie chart to select it. Click the Chart Tools Design tab to switch to formatting the artwork. Click the Shape Outline button and choose Weight > 3 pt to thicken the lines **B**.

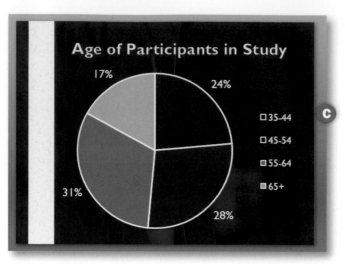

2. Prep the Chart—Text

If the chart contains labels, be sure they appear outside of the chart (otherwise the animation may cover the numbers). Choose the Chart Tools Layout tab from the Ribbon and click the Data Labels button and choose Outside End **A** to move the data labels. Choose the Home tab in the Ribbon to access the type controls. Click on the percentage numbers to select them. Click the Increase Font Size button in the Font group two times **B**. Then select the legend of the chart and enlarge it by clicking the Increase Font Size button twice again **C**.

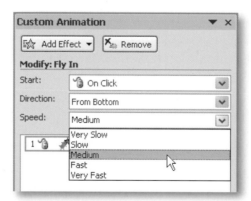

3. Add an Entrance Effect

Now that the chart's appearance has been optimized it can be animated. Click on the pie chart to select it, and then click the Animations tab in the Ribbon. If the Custom Animation task pane is not visible, click the Custom Animation button in the Animations group. Click the Add Effect button and choose Entrance > Fly In. The chart now flies in from the bottom of the screen, but the effect can be customized. Before animating pie segments individually, change the rate of the effect. Click the Speed list and set the rate to Medium.

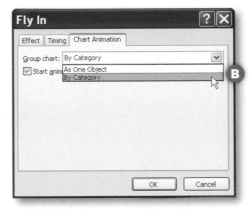

4. Animate Elements Independently

To create animation with impact, you can set the pie segments to build one at a time. This will allow the presenter to discuss each group independently. In the Custom Animation task pane click the drop-down menu on the first animation and choose Effect Options **A**. A new window opens with controls for the Fly In effect. Click the Chart Animation tab and change Group chart to By Category **B** and uncheck the Start animation by drawing the chart background box and clicking OK.

5. Adjust Animation Direction and Timings

In the Custom Animation task pane, click the double arrows to expand the contents of the animation effect (this will allow you to view and modify each animation independently) **A**. Click on the first animation (Chart 3: Category 1) and change its direction to From Top-Right in the Direction list **B**. Select the remaining segments and set each one to the following: Category 2, Bottom-Right; Category 3, Bottom-Left; and Category 4, Top-Left.

6. Preview the Animation

To view the changes in animation you have two choices. You can launch the presentation from the current slide by pressing Shift+F5 or you can click the Play button at the bottom of the Custom Animation pane. 🔲

Using GIF Files

Another way to add animation to a slide is to use an animated GIF file (pronounced jif). The GIF or (Graphics Interchange Format) was first introduced by CompuServe in 1987. The format was further modified in 1989 to add animation support. The format only allows 256 colors per frame, and this color limitation can make the images appear coarse and grainy. There are lots of places to find GIF files (and you can even create your own). If you'd like some animation in your slide show, consider the GIF file as an option.

Clip Art on Office Online

At first glance, you wouldn't know that the Clip Art browser supports animated GIF files. That's because Microsoft uses a different name. If you click the drop-down menu under Results should be, you can specify to search only for Movies. You can now perform key-word searches for animated graphics.

Searching Online

T I P

Change the Color. If a GIF file doesn't match your presentation's color then don't worry. Just select the GIF on your slide and switch to the Picture Tools Format tab in the Ribbon. Click the Recolor button in the Adjust group and make your desired color change.

There is no shortage of manufacturers to choose from for GIF animations. A quick Web search will reveal plenty of options for any budget range. The sites with the most options and highest quality tend to cost more, but you should have no problems finding results. Be sure to shop around, as our searches found a ton of pricing options from pay-per-item to monthly membership plans. Be sure to weigh your options before making purchases. In fact, before buying anything, you may want to send a preview Web link if someone else must approve the presentation.

Here are a few sites to explore: www.gifanimations.com. www.animationfactory.com, www.gif.com.

Making Your Own

I N S I G H T

GIF Versus SWF. There are two major Web formats for animation GIF as well as the newer SWF (or Flash) format. Because Flash files are often used for video, we covered Flash integration back in Chapter 4. If you need to use a SWF animation you can flip back and follow those steps.

If you are artistically inclined, you can use most graphics and animation software programs to create GIF files. We frequently use Adobe After Effects for very advanced animation files. Another option is Adobe Photoshop, which has very rich Web support. For more on animating using Photoshop be sure to check out *How to Wow with Photoshop CS2 for the Web* by Jan Kabili and Colin Smith. ▨

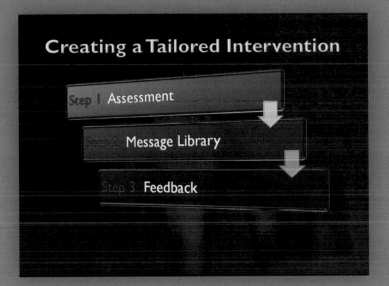

Animating SmartArt

Animating Diagrams Is Easy with SmartArt

1. Choose the Slide to Animate

This presentation contains three pieces of SmartArt that can be animated. To animate SmartArt for maximum impact, use a reveal style build, in which each element is added in progression to the slide. To practice animating SmartArt, switch to slide 20 in the Slides list in your chapter project.

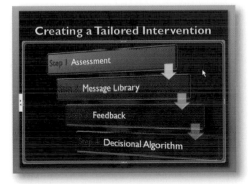

2. Select the SmartArt to Animate

With SmartArt you need to be aware when you click. For example, clicking on a box will put the graphic into editing mode. Instead, click just outside the graphic so a selection box occurs. The border around the SmartArt indicates that is selected (and can also be used to size and reposition the artwork).

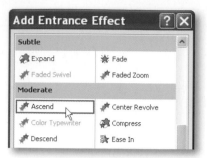

3. Add a Custom Animation

Click the Animations tab in the Ribbon to access control over animation. If the Custom Animation task pane is not visible, click the Custom Animation button in the Animations group. Click the Add Effect button and choose Entrance > More Effects. In the new window scroll down to the Moderate category and choose Ascend. A preview of the bars rising into place plays back. Click OK to apply the effect.

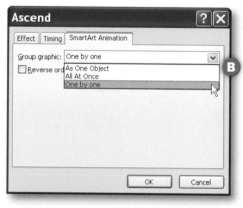

4. Convert the Custom Animation to a Build

In order to better control the Custom Animation, click the drop-down menu to the right of its name and choose Effect Options **A**. In the new window, click the SmartArt Animation tab. Change Group graphic to One by one (make sure the Reverse order box is unchecked) **B**. Click OK to apply the animation.

T I P

Faster Options. You can double-click on an effect in order to access its Effect Options. This shortcut can save you time.

5. Preview the Animation

In order to see the animation in action, you can click the Play button at the bottom of the Custom Animation task pane. The four boxes should slide into place one after another. If you'd like additional practice, you can animate the SmartArt on slides 16 and 23 as well. ▦

The Theory of Transitions

Presenters are oddly attracted to transitions (or wipes) between slides. This obsession is further fed by the fact that all presentation (and for that matter video) software pushes transitions as one of the top features. Are transitions helpful? Certainly. Do most presenters improperly use them? Most definitely! Restraint is key when choosing transitions.

When to Use Transitions

Most presenters think they should use a transition between every slide. This view assumes that you want something to signify a change of ideas to the audience. This theory works well if you remember that a cut (in which one shot instantly changes to another) is also considered a transition. Problems arise when presenters think of transitions as fun and begin to overly rely on them to add interest to their slide shows. A better approach is to determine how dramatic a change is needed. Ask yourself the following:

- How well do the adjoining slides fit together?

- What is the response you want from the audience? A continuation of thought, or an entirely new topic of discussion?

- Does the transition feel right, or is it jarring?

Yes, every slide will have a transition, and that transition will usually be a cut. Transition abuse is a common mistake of amateur presenters. When we call someone an amateur we don't base it on how long the speaker has used software, rather on his or her lack of experience in standing in front of a live audience and delivering effective presentations.

Transition Speed

Virtually every transition in PowerPoint can have its speed changed (the exception being the Cut). Transitions give you three speed options: slow, medium, or fast. It is generally good to set your transitions to a consistent speed by using the same speed setting.

Transition Categories

PowerPoint 2007 offers 59 built-in transitions organized into the six categories listed below. These transitions are frequently slight variations upon each other (such as left-right-top-bottom).

- No Transition—There is only one transition in this category, and while it is named No Transition, it is often referred to as a cut. There is also a Cut in the Fade and Dissolves category and it functions in the same way as No Transition.

- Fades and Dissolves—In this category there are five transitions, all of which will either fade from one image to another or temporarily fade to black and move into the next slide. This category tends to be subtle and is well suited for most presentations.

- Wipes—The wipes category contains 32 different transitions. A wipe uses a shape such as a square or circle to reveal the incoming image. Wipes tend to be more dramatic than Fades or Dissolves and should be used less frequently.

- Push and Cover—This category offers 12 options. A Push uses one slide to push the old slide off the screen, much like trains on a track. A Cover pushes a new slide on top of the old, obscuring it in the process.

- Stripes and Bars—There are six different Stripes or Bars wipes to choose from. These use strips or checkerboard patterns to mix two images together.

- Random—The Random category uses either random horizontal or vertical bars to create the wipe. Additionally, a third option, called Random Transition, will pick from all the built-in options.

Limiting Styles

When using transitions, it's important to keep your style consistent. Many presenters will try and use a different transition on every slide. While this is technically possible, it is a very bad idea. When choosing wipes, you'll want them to be complementary (such as a Wipe Left and Wipe Right). By keeping your transitions consistent, the presentation will feel more professional and cohesive. This advice can be summed up by using the words of the wise Mr. Miyagi of *The Karate Kid* fame: "Wax on… wax off." 🎬

Adding Transitions to Slides

Create Fluid Motion Between Slides

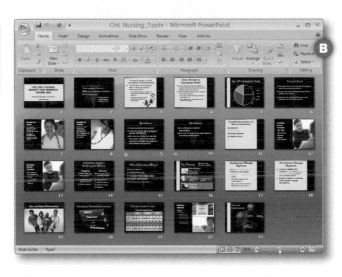

1. Switch to Slide Sorter View

The easiest way to apply slide transitions is to take a global view of your entire presentation. One easy way to do this is to switch to the Slide Sorter view by clicking the Slide Sorter icon on the bottom of the window **A**. Then adjust the Zoom slider so you can see all 23 slides in your window **B**. Depending upon the size of your computer monitor, you may need to use a different zoom level.

2. Apply a Global Transition

Generally you can apply a global transition to all of your slides and then modify individual transitions based on need. This global transition should be subtle (such as a Cut or Fade Smoothly). Press Ctrl+A to select all of your slides. Click the Animations tab and click the Fade Smoothly button in the Transitions to This Slide. A transition is applied to each slide; its existence is indicated by the star icon beneath each slide's thumbnail.

3. Adjust the Speed

Since your slides are still selected, it is easy to apply a global speed change. Choose the Transition Speed drop-down menu and set the speed to Medium. The icons of your slides animate as the transitions are updated across all slides.

C A U T I O N

Hear No Evil. You may have noticed the Transition Sound option in the Animations tab—don't use it! If you really feel the need to apply the Applause sound effect, your presentation needs more than a sound effect. That Whoosh sound? Lets just say that reliance on gimmicks makes for a bad presentation.

4. Adjust Individual Transitions

While the global transition works for most slides, you'll often want to modify specific slides to customize your transitions. First, deselect all slides by clicking in an empty area in the slide sorter. You can then select multiple slides by Ctrl+clicking on their thumbnails. To practice, select slides 1, 2, 7, 8, 13, and 19. In the Animations tab click Fade Through Black to apply a new transition.

5. Remove Unwanted Transitions

Earlier you created an Entrance and Exit build for bulleted text on slides 9 and 10. These two slides do not need a transition in between them. Select slide 10 in the Slide Sorter then click the No Transition button in the Animations tab.

6. Watch the Show

Now that the presentation has had animation added you should watch it all the way through. Click the Slide Show tab to access the controls. Click the From Beginning button to view your show from the start. Click the space bar to advance your slide show through each animation. When you are finished with the presentation, press the escape key to exit the show. ▧

T I P

Using Hyperlinks as Transitions. If you want to link to another slide in your presentation, you can use a hyperlink. You can either select an object (like a piece of SmartArt or a shape) or highlight a word of text. Then choose the Insert tab in the Ribbon and click on Hyperlink in the Links group. You can then choose to use a Place in This Document. Select a slide from the list and click OK. Hyperlinks can jump to any slide in the document, but the transitions on the slide will be ignored.

Using Third Party Transitions

PowerPoint can be modified through several different software add-ins. These modifications to the program are meant to increase functionality and enable customization. These tools are made by a variety of software companies, and you must purchase them if you want to add them to your toolbox. Lets explore the case for and against transition add-ins.

The Case for Transition Add-Ins

Simply put, if you want fancier and bigger transitions, then you'll need to look at third-party plug-ins. We have tried several of them out and most do what they advertise. With little effort, your slides will be spinning, flying, and even morphing into new shapes. If your client or company wants fancy transitions then you'll need to look beyond the built-in tools. The library of available effects is impressive, and they work well for attention-demanding situations like self-running presentations for trade shows. Keep in mind, though, that you can quickly spend more on add-ins than you paid for PowerPoint to begin with.

The Case Against Transition Add-Ins

The use of add-in transitions is very machine dependant. Many of them require robust graphics cards and system memory in order to play back. This means you'll need a fast computer (and likely will need to bring your own with you). Additionally, the add-ins require that software be loaded on both the machine where the show was created as well as the one it was played back on. This can require lots of installing and technical challenges in the field. Another issue is stability. Complex 3-D effects greatly increase the chance of an application crash, which can be deadly in front of a live audience. The final issue is just plain good taste. While we have been pretty transparent about our feeling on gaudy transitions, it bears repeating—keep things simple and clean. After all, do you really need that 3-D animated-dolphin wipe? Wow your audience with good design and good information, not glitter and sound effects. ▥

7

DELIVERING THE PRESENTATION

How to Take a Presentation on the Road and Share it with Others

CONGRATULATIONS. YOU'VE pulled two all-nighters, scrambled all over the planet to find the perfect images, set up your master slides with the right fonts, populated each slide with the information you'll need, and your ready to go. Wait! Don't cram your laptop in your bag and race out the door—there is still work to be done. Prepping the file for delivery is the final (and some might say the most important) stage in building your presentation. We've been on both sides. We've been called upon to do last minute presentations and we've also been the on-site crew at events where we were presented with a floppy disk seconds before the speaker walked on stage. Yes, a floppy disk. The answer to both scenarios was to fall back on the old scout motto: Be prepared. We'll show you some techniques to help prevent these showtime slip-ups and talk about what it takes to get your show on the road.

Reviewing

Let's be honest, most of the time presentations are tweaked until the last minute, leaving barely enough time to save them, much less review them for technical soundness. We know. We've been there. You have to think of it this way, what is more painful—not getting in that last tweak, or standing in front of your coworkers and clients with a massive red X behind you where your image was supposed to be? It could only be worse if you handed off a presentation to your boss and then discovered that there was a typo in his name on the intro slide and that the product demo movie didn't play on his laptop.

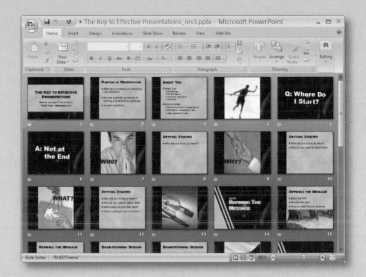

Collecting

Making sure that the presentation you created is seen the same way by your intended audience is critical. If there is a missing font, text can wrap strangely or words can disappear altogether. If the presentation is e-mailed to a presenter without the critical movie and audio files attached, the presenter will have nothing to show. Remember, some things are embedded in the presentation and some are not.

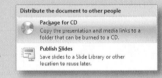

Publishing

How is your presentation going to be delivered? Will you need to prep it for a one-time show, or will it be delivered in multiple mediums in different situations? Is it important for your audience to walk away with the information that was delivered in the presentation? Will it need to be projected from an event computer, printed

out, viewed on the Web during a teleconference, or run in a trade-show booth on a loop? Once these questions are answered, you can prepare your files for the right delivery vehicles.

Transferring

Ok, you've proofed, printed, and tested the presentation thoroughly and it looks good and works great on your computer. The next step is being able to get it to where it needs to be. Even if you plan on presenting it from the same computer it was created on, you'll still need a backup plan because Murphy's Law applies to PowerPoint and to presentations in particular more than we'd like to think.

Final Proofing

Before you send a presentation out the door, you must closely examine it for errors and inconsistencies. We find that no matter how much scrutiny and care is applied during the construction of a presentation, errors still manage to sneak in. But with some care, determination, and teamwork you can deal with embarrassing mistakes in the comfort of your cubicle rather than on center stage.

TIP

High Tech and Product Names.
Brand names, technology words, product names, or proper nouns may be missing from the built-in dictionary. If you know a word is correct, click the Add button within the Spelling dialog box.

Spell Checking

PowerPoint includes a built-in spell check that can be used to catch most spelling errors. In fact, you'll occasionally see that words are underlined with a jagged red line. That line indicates a misspelling (or a word that has not yet been added to the PowerPoint's dictionary). The Spell check can be invoked by choosing the Review tab in the Ribbon and clicking the Spelling button. Alternately, you can right-click an underlined word and pick a replacement from a list of suggestions.

Grammar Checking

Regular users of Microsoft Word will be surprised and disappointed that there is no built-in grammar check for PowerPoint. If you need to clean up a large portion of text and want to harness a grammar check command, then you'll need to use the shared Office clipboard. You can select a block of text and choose to copy it (Ctrl+C) to your clipboard. Switch to Word and paste the text into a new document. There you can run a grammar check by choosing the Review tab and clicking Spelling & Grammar. The text can then be copied back to your clipboard so it can be returned to PowerPoint.

Viewing as Grayscale for Contrast

Not all slide color combinations are well suited for presentations. Some color combinations lack adequate contrast, which can make a slide hard for the audience to comprehend. This can be especially problematic for older audience members, those with poor vision, or those who may be color-blind. Printing your slides as a grayscale image first is a great way to check for proper contrast.

> **INSIGHT**
>
> **Color Contrast.** When you are comparing colors and combinations, it may be difficult to understand where contrast problems come from. Remember there are three components to a color—Hue, Saturation, and Luminance. Hue is the color of the spectrum that is used, Saturation is the intensity of that color, and Lightness is the presence of white or black. When Hue and Saturation are removed it is easy to see problems in contrast.

Proofing a Hard Copy

One point we make frequently is that it's hard to catch a mistake if you don't change your setting. Mistakes made while typing on a computer are much harder to spot when proofreading on a computer. The best way to spot errors is to go the traditional route when proofing. Print out a hard (paper) copy of your slides to mark up, then take a red pen to the page and look for errors. This method of catching mistakes really does work.

Having a Friend Help You Out

Related to catching errors on your own is calling upon a peer to help you out. If a presentation is really important you should really enlist another set of eyes. We find that a coworker can often find errors that we miss. Don't be afraid to ask for help; it will only benefit your presentation.

Taking It to the Big Screen

We like to do a click-through of a presentation on a large screen in order to look for errors. By running your presentation on a projector, you can create a situation where errors stand out easily. This "tech rehearsal" is a great time to look for glitches, missing transitions, and broken links. Actors hold several dress rehearsals before opening night; the goal is to work out all of the kinks in the show before there is a live audience. Needless to say, this is a very good idea in the world of presentations. ▥

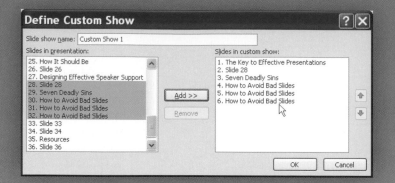

Customizing the Show

Use One Presentation to Create Custom Shows

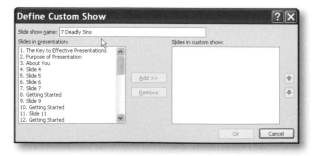

1. Prepare Your Files

In order to complete this exercise (and others in this chapter) you'll need to copy the files to your local computer. From the project CD-ROM, open the HTW Project Files folder and copy the Chapter 7 folder to your local hard drive. This folder contains all of the files needed for this chapter. Open the file CH7_The_Key_to_Effective_Presentations.pptx.

2. Create a New Custom Show

In your Ribbon, Select the Slide Show tab. In the Start Slide Show Group, select the Custom Slide Show button and then the Custom Shows button **A**. The Custom Shows window will open. Click the New button to create a Custom Show from your existing slides **B**.

3. Define Your Custom Show

The Define Custom Show window is divided into two sections—the Slides in presentation window and the Slides in custom show window. In the Slide show name box, type in 7 Deadly Sins (always, name your custom shows to ensure that you'll be able to identify them quickly).

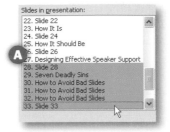

4. Customize Your Slides

Select Slides 1, 28, 29, 30, 31, 32, and 33 and then click the Add button (if you hold down the control key after you click slide one, you can select each additional slide as well) **A**.

To reorder the slides in your custom show, select the slide that you would like to move and then click the up or down arrows to change its order in the show **B**. Click OK.

5. Test Your Show

After you click OK, the Custom shows window will open, showing you the custom shows that are available. Select the 7 Deadly Sins show and then click the Show button. Your presentation will begin. Click through your custom show to ensure that each slide that you've selected in the Define Custom Show window is indeed displayed in order.

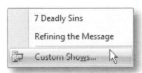

6. Build Multiple Custom Shows

Now that you've tested your custom show, go back and repeat the process for another custom show. In the Slide Show tab, click the Custom Shows button. Then 7 Deadly Sins and the additional show that you've just created will appear as options in the drop-down window.

Now it is possible to have a complete corporate overview, with a custom show for each division or each product, or an entire semester broken down into custom shows for each lesson plan.

7. Hide slides

Another way to customize a presentation quickly is to hide selected slides. It's useful to hide slides when you're not sure if you'll have enough time to go into detail. Then if a question is asked or if you have more time than expected, they are there for you to call up. Select a slide thumbnail on the left of your main viewing window and right-click it. Select Hide Slide from the content menu. The thumbnail will fade, and a line will cut through the slide number, indicating that the slide is hidden.

8. Run the Presentation with Hidden Slides

Go to the Slide Show tab in the ribbon. Click the From Beginning button in the Start Slide Show Group. Advance through the presentation. The presentation will run as if the slides that you've hidden do not exist.

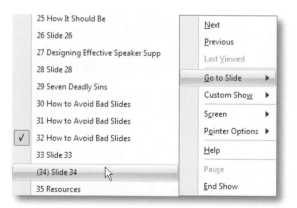

9. Show Hidden Slides

If you need to refer to a hidden slide, there is an easy way to do it. With the presentation still running in Slide Show mode, right-click anywhere on the screen. A menu will appear. Click the Go to Slide button. All of your slide titles will appear (it's quickly apparent why it's important to make sure each slide is named here). You'll notice that the slide numbers that are hidden appear within parentheses. Select a hidden slide. The hidden slide will be temporarily unhidden. You'll also notice that you can access your custom shows on the fly from this menu.

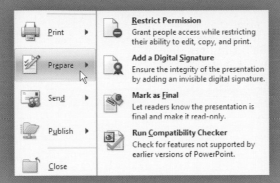

Making the Presentation Mobile

There's a Lot You Can Do to Get a Presentation Ready

1. Open the Presentation You Want to Prep

In order to optimize a presentation, you'll need to have the document open. You can use the same project file that you opened earlier in this chapter. Be sure to have all fonts active, and run the presentation off a disk that can be modified (in other words, not a CD-ROM).

2. Save a Copy of the Presentation

Before you significantly modify the presentation, it's a good idea to back up your work. An easy way to do that is to use the Save As command. In the ribbon, click the Office Button. Choose Save As > PowerPoint Presentation and rename the file. We recommend keeping the existing name but adding an additional word, Optimized.

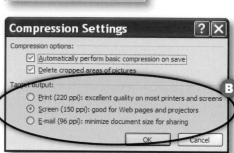

3. Optimize Image Size

A presentation file's size is often greatly affected by the digital photos inside it. Many users drop in full-quality images direct from their digital cameras or scanners. These files are higher quality, as they are often intended for printing, which requires the extra information to make a clean print. Screen graphics, however, are much lower quality. By optimizing the images in your presentation, you can make the size smaller, which in turn will make slides load faster and make it easier to move a presentation to another machine.

In order to optimize images, you must have an active selection. Switch to slide 4 and select the photo of a runner. Click the Format tab in the Ribbon. In the Adjust Group, click the Compress Picture button **A**. A new dialog box opens; click Options to access greater controls. You have several options **B**. We usually choose to optimize for screen at 150 ppi. When ready, you can choose to apply the compression to the selected photos only or to all of the photos in the presentation.

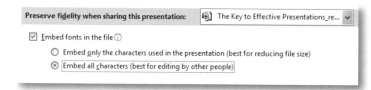

4. Embed the Fonts

In order to avoid font errors on your presentation machine, you'll need to ensure that all fonts you've used make the journey too. PowerPoint can embed fonts into a presentation, which will allow you to open and modify your slides on another machine without having the font loaded.

To enable font embedding, click the Office Button in the Ribbon. Choose the Save category, then enable Embed fonts in the file. We recommend choosing the Embed all characters option for greater flexibility.

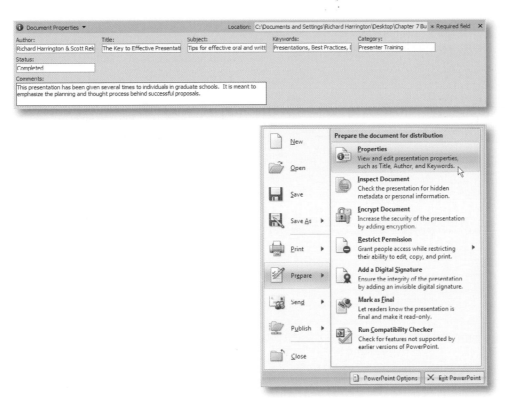

5. Adjust Document Properties

Before you send the presentation out the door, you might want to put your name on it. By modifying the document properties you can insert biographical information that makes it easier to claim ownership of a slide show.

Click the Office Button in the Ribbon and choose Prepare > Properties. A pane opens above the slide presentation allowing you to enter several pieces of information about the slide show. This can be helpful when sharing the presentation or sifting for content. If you click the drop-down menu next to Document Properties you can access Advanced Properties including statistics for your show's content and a list of review and approvals. You can click the X to close the Document Properties pane.

6. Inspect the Document

If you are concerned about releasing personal information with your slide show, then you should let PowerPoint inspect it to clean the file. Click the Office Button in the Ribbon and choose Prepare > Inspect Document. If you have any unsaved changes, PowerPoint will prompt you to save the file first. In the Document Inspector window, ensure that all tasks are checked so they will be performed, then click the Inspect button. For this presentation file Power-Point will warn you that you have comments attached and give you the option to remove them (in this case, just click cancel and leave them intact).

Microsoft Office PowerPoint Compatibility Checker [?] [X]

Because some of the features in this presentation are not supported by versions of PowerPoint earlier than PowerPoint 2007, the features will be lost or degraded if you save the presentation in an earlier format.

Summary   Number of occurrences

This object will no longer be editable.   11

Help

Customized prompt text in custom layouts will be removed.   1

Help

☑ Check compatibility when saving in PowerPoint 97-2003 formats.

OK

INSIGHT

Why Go Back? You may wonder why you'd save a PowerPoint 2003 format presentation. The simple answer is that you may not have a choice. If you are unsure of which version of the software will be available to you on the presentation computer then backwards compatibility is a must. After all, not all companies (or individuals) upgrade the software as fast as you (the smart and industrious individual that you are).

7. Check Compatibility

PowerPoint 2007 adds new features (such as SmartArt and character styles) that are not fully compatible with older versions. Click the Office Button in the Ribbon and choose Prepare > Compatibility Checker (the presentation may take a few moments to prepare itself, so don't worry about the pause).

After the check is completed, PowerPoint will generate a series of warnings about saving to an older format. Usually these warnings mean that you will lose the ability to edit certain features of your slide if you save to a backwards-compatible file. You can click OK to close the list of warnings.

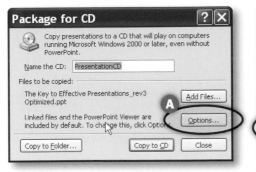

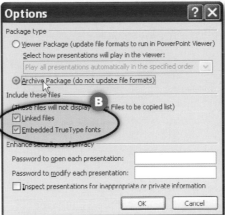

8. Gather Source Files & Package for CD

Now that you have proofed and tested your presentation file it is time to bundle that presentation so you can move it to another machine. If you've followed our advice about keeping project files together in one folder, then you should be able to just copy that folder to some form of removable magnetic or optical media (see Mobile Media next in this chapter). However, if you are a little less organized, PowerPoint offers a helping hand. You can click the Office Button and choose Prepare > Package for CD. A warning box appears to let you know that a backwards-compatible file will also be created, click OK to continue and the Package for CD window opens. Click the Options button **A** to specify a few advanced settings. Make sure that both Linked files and Embedded True Type fonts boxes are checked to gather more source materials **B**. If you'd like you can choose to Archive Package, which will simply gather the files and not make a new backwards-compatible file. When ready, click OK. You can now choose to Copy to Folder or Copy to CD depending upon your needs. We usually use Copy to Folder and then move the files manually to a target drive. Click Copy to Folder to complete the archive procedure. You now must set a folder name as well as a destination, then click OK. Another box asks you if you are sure you want to complete the task and sure that you trust all of the sources; you can go ahead and click Yes. When the task is completed, you must click Close to close the Package for CD window. ▥

Mobile Media

Successfully taking a presentation from your cubicle, corner office, classroom, place of worship, or garage out to the masses will require a basic knowledge of mobile media. Knowing the type of media to carry that message is half the battle. You'll also need to make sure that all of the files are transferred properly with security options enabled (if necessary). As with any new media, before purchasing any new hardware, it's best to check out all of the customer reviews.

Using Mini USB Flash Drives

KRZYSCIN/ISTOCKPHOTO

The ability of this device to put several gigabytes of information on a drive that is roughly the size of your thumb makes going mobile a snap. A flash drive works the same way your internal drives work. Just drag and drop, copy and paste, or save to one of these mini-drives and you're ready to plug it into a backup computer if something goes wrong (make sure to save a version as PowerPoint 97-2003 as well). Everyone who uses a computer should have one of these. It will get you out of a jam, we promise. These drives are small and easy to lose; they are also prone to getting bent or damaged. Look for drives that are rugged. One manufacturer claims that its drive will withstand 2000 pounds of pressure. We've seen a car drive over one, and it still worked. If your information is confidential, make sure to password protect the presentation and the drive itself (if it comes with software to do so).

CAUTION

Protect Your Investment. A USB flash drive will protrude from your laptop or desktop and make it easy to accidentally bump into it and damage your internal USB card. It's a good practice to remove the drive immediately after the files have been transferred.

Using Portable Hard Drives

KRZYSIEK Z POCZTY/ISTOCKPHOTO

If you have a lot of video content, software to demo, or generally more information than will fit on a mini USB Flash drive, a portable hard drive can be a good option. The same rules apply for file security with these, make sure to encrypt or password-protect sensitive data. What you should look for in a portable drive is capacity, durability, bus-powered and included backup, and encryption software. Bus-powered drives require no power adapter to plug into an outlet. This will allow you to use the drive when your laptop is running off of battery alone. Some drives include a protective carrying case as well.

TIP

iPod = Portable Hard Drive. Remember that your iPod can also work as a portable hard drive. It can run a presentation using just a few accessories, including a dock, remote, and A/V cable. Just save your slides as JPEGs and advance through them in photo slide show mode. How cool is that?

Copying to CD and DVD

CDs and DVDs are inexpensive ways to backup and transfer your presentations. Using the Package for CD command mentioned earlier in this chapter is the best method to ensure that all the needed files are copied onto your CD. If you would like to archive the presentation to a DVD you can package the presentation to a folder and then use your normal DVD burning software to copy that folder to a DVD. If you would like to make a DVD of the presentation that will run from a computer with a DVD drive and most standard DVD players, there are third party software packages available that will allow you to do this. One option, from Wondershare, is called PPT2DVD. Keep in mind that not all laptops will have DVD players, so choose your media wisely.

E-mailing a Presentation

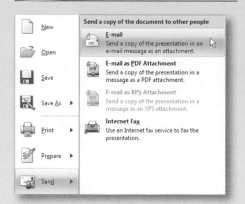

Inevitably you need to to e-mail a presentation for review purposes or to send it to someone that wasn't able to attend. You can speed up the process by e-mailing the presentation directly from PowerPoint. Under the Office Button drop-down menu, click the Send button. Then click the E-mail button to configure who will receive the presentation. Keep in mind that your e-mail profile must be configured properly in your control panel for this function to work properly.

> ### CAUTION
>
> **Optimize Before E-mailing.** Make sure to optimize your presentation for the smallest file size before attempting to e-mail it. Many e-mail providers will only allow a small file size to transfer through their system. Even if large file sizes are allowed, many people will not appreciate the added wait time that you've caused them when they attempt to download and view their mail.

Transferring to a Laptop

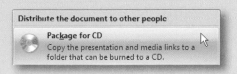

The most efficient way to transfer files from a desktop computer to a laptop is by using the Package for CD option that we mentioned earlier. By selecting the Copy to Folder option you can save the presentation and all of the linked files to a folder on your desktop. Then use a portable media device such as a mini USB Flash Drive or a portable hard drive to transfer the files to your laptop. ▦

Creating and Customizing Handouts

When Your Audience Needs to Walk Away with Information

1. Open the Presentation to Format the Handout Master

Let's go back to the presentation that we've been using for this chapter. Make sure to open the version that you've copied from the project CD. Select the View tab and then select the Handout Master button in the Presentation Views group.

2. Decide How Many Slides Per Page

You'll need to determine how many slides per page your presentation will require. If most of your slides consist of bullet points set in 25-point or higher text, you can get away with six slides per page. If your presentation has slides with a lot of text, or charts with small text, or detailed graphics, you might want to consider one or two slides per page. For this presentation, click the Slides Per Page button and click the 6 Slides button in the Page Setup Group.

3. Determine What to Include

Under the Placeholders group, select the attributes that you would like to have printed on each page of your handouts. You can modify the header to display your company name and the footer to display the content of your presentation by clicking in the appropriate text field in the main window. The page numbers will be set automatically for you.

4. Prepare for Printout

Under the Page Setup group, select the Page Setup button. Click the Slides sized for: drop-down menu and select Letter Paper (8.5 x 11 in). In the Orientation group, select Landscape under the Slides area and Portrait under the Notes, handouts & outline area.

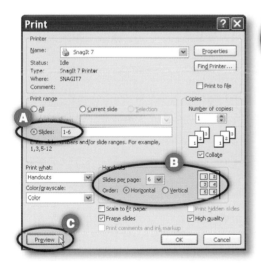

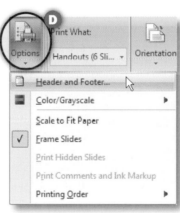

5. Print

Click the Office Button and the Print button from the submenu. In the Print window select your default printer. Select slides 1–6 in the Print range group **A**. In the Handouts group, select 6 in the Slides per page menu, and the order should be horizontal **B**. Check the High Quality box and the Frame slides box. Next, hit the Preview button **C**. Inside the Print Preview tab, click the Options button in the Print group to reveal more options before you commit to the Print button **D**.

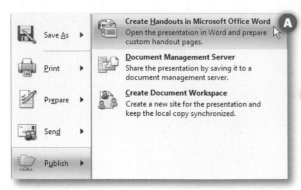

INSIGHT

Useful Handouts. Make sure to take advantage of the option of providing more information in the notes fields of your handouts. Your audience will appreciate a written explanation of your bullet points when they are reviewing them after the presentation.

6. Need More Control? Save as a Word Document

If you would like to have a little more control over the look or content in a handout, you can save the handouts as Word documents. Click the Office Button and then click the Publish button in the drop-down menu. Then select the Create Handouts in Microsoft Office Word button **A**. In the Send To Microsoft Office Word window select Notes below slides in the Page Layout group and Paste link in the Add slides to Microsoft Office Word document group **B**. Power-Point will now automate the creation of a fully editable Microsoft Word Presentation Handout. ▥

Creating a Kiosk Presentation

When the Show Must Go On Without You

1. It's All in the Timing

Kiosk Presentations can be used at trade show booths, company reception areas, museums, and anywhere you might need a presentation to run without having someone there to interact with it. The first step to creating this kind of presentation is to get the slide timing down. Open the Key to Effective Presentations show that you copied to your hard drive earlier. In the Slide Show tab, click the Rehearse Timings button in the Set Up group. Be prepared to jump to step 2 quickly.

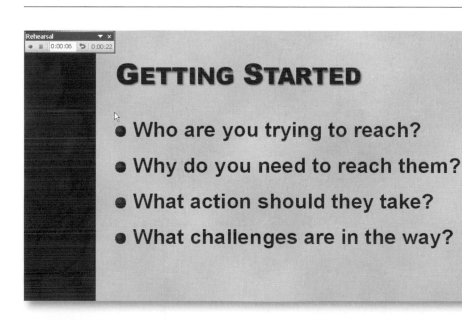

2. Time Each Slide

The presentation will open with a Rehearsal Tool bar in the upper right corner. Slowly read each slide twice and then click the Next button to advance to the next slide. Repeat this action for each slide. When a slide has a full screen photograph or a photo with just a few words use your best judgment on how long it should stay visible. The more complex the photo, the longer it should stay up. Keep in mind that if it stays up too long, people may lose interest and assume that the presentation has stalled. We've found that about 5 seconds is usually enough for most photos.

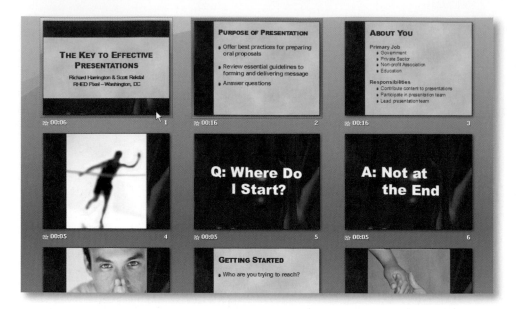

3. Determine Total Time of Show

Once the presentation has completed and you've timed out each slide, a dialog box will appear asking you if you would like to keep the timings that you've set when you view the slide show. Select Yes. Your presentation will then open in the Slide Sorter view with the timings that you've attributed to each slide appearing to the bottom left. (The little star icon represents a transition that has been set up for that slide. You can click that to see a preview.)

4. Set Up Slide Show

Click the Set Up Slide Show button in the Set Up group. This will open a Set Up Show window that will allow you to set the preferences needed for the presentation to run in Kiosk mode. In the Show type group select the Browsed at a kiosk (full screen) option. In the Advance slides group, select Using timings, if present option.

5. Start the Show and Head Out for Coffee

In the Slide Show tab click From Beginning button in the Start Slide Show group. This will begin the presentation in kiosk mode and loop it continuously until you hit the escape button. The multimedia options that we discussed in Chapter 4 might be able to spice up your presentation in your absence. ⌨

CAUTION

Narrated Presentations. Yes, you can record a narration for your slides in PowerPoint. However, you can turn a good presentation into an unwatchable disaster with a poorly recorded narration. Unless your 100 percent confident in your recording equipment and voice talent, you're better off without it.

Implementing Rehearsed Timings

Imagine a world where your presentation runs on its own, with little need for human intervention. Does that sound scary or helpful? The answer may be "it depends." If you navigate to the Slide Show tab in the Ribbon, you can click the Rehearse Timings button. This will launch your slide show so you can then navigate through it in real time. When you click to trigger a bullet build or slide transition, PowerPoint memorizes timings for the slide. Knowing when to harness Rehearsed Timings will save you time and potential embarrassment.

When to Use Rehearsed Timings

There are some very good reasons to use Rehearsed Timings. Previously, you used them when creating a self-running kiosk style presentation. In a similar fashion, you may need to repeatedly give a presentation in less than ideal situations (such as at a trade-show booth). In this scenario, the presentation is likely to be highly scripted, with little or no audience interaction. The use of Rehearsed Timings will allow you to create a slide presentation that runs on its own, thus freeing the presenter to focus more on their talk and less on clicking. We recommend Rehearsed Timings for those situations when a presenter will not be present or when the presenter is unable to focus on the operation of the slide show.

When Not to Use Rehearsed Timings

JEFFREY SMITH//ISTOCKPHOTO

There is nothing more boring than a presentation when the presenter is literally on autopilot—merely a robot (or extension of the computer) and totally oblivious to the audience. The purpose of PowerPoint is to serve as speaker support, not speaker replacement. If you remove your ability to interact with the audience, to read facial expressions, to adjust the flow due to audience response or questions, then you are greatly impacting the quality of your presentation. The role of the presenter is to evoke a change in thinking or action; you'll need as much connection as possible to bring this about. ▥

Using the Presenter View

PowerPoint 2007 adds a new option called Presenter View which gives a presenter more options when running a presentation from one computer (like a laptop) and sending it to another screen (like a projector). Presenter View gives you powerful options, like thumbnails for selecting slides out of sequence, as well as a Preview text for the next slide and the ability to see your speaker notes on the presenter's computer (but not the main screen).

Requirements for Presenter View

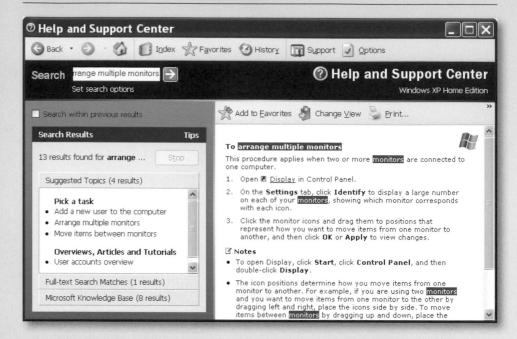

In order to harness the Presenter View you must meet certain technical requirements:

1. PowerPoint 2007 must be loaded on the computer.

2. The computer needs to be able to support multiple monitors. This may mean a second video card for a desktop computer (but laptops usually have this feature built-in).

3. Multiple monitor support for your computer must be turned on. (The exact way will vary depending on the version of the Operating System you have loaded.) A search for "arrange multiple monitors" in the Help and Support Center will give you detailed instructions.

Enabling Presenter View

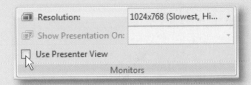

Turning on the Presenter View is easy. Ensure that the second monitor is active. Then in the Ribbon click the Slide Show tab, and from the Monitors group check the box next to the Use Presenter View option. When you start the Slide Show (F5) the Presenter View will be visible.

An Overview of Presenter View

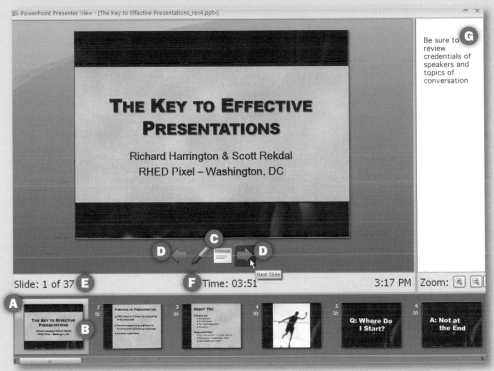

There are several icons and buttons you'll need to use to navigate the Presenter View. The figure above illustrates the major controls that you'll want to use.

A A thumbnail list of slides that you can use to navigate through your slide show.

B The active slide that the audience is viewing.

C The ability to annotate a slide.

D Forward and backward buttons.

E The slide number of the current slide.

F The elapsed time (in minutes and seconds) since beginning the presentation.

G The speaker's notes, which you can use as a memory jogger. 🎹

Saving Files as Still Images or PDFs

It Is Possible to Export Various Graphic Files Including PDF

1. Load the PDF Plug-in

The PDF is an excellent format for sharing your presentation with others, as it allows for easy viewing with the free Adobe Reader. The files maintain the exact appearance of the slide and cannot be easily modified by the end user. While PowerPoint does not support PDF files out of the box, adding the capability is very easy. The location of this plug-in can vary on Microsoft's Web site. The easiest way to find the plug-in is to launch the help menu (F1) and type PDF in the search box. A detailed help article with a direct link to the PDF installer will be first on the list. Download the installer and run the executable file.

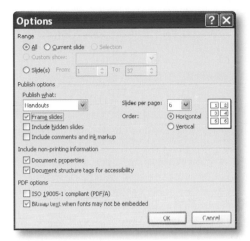

2. Save the PDF File

Once the plug-in is installed, saving a PDF is easy. Work with the sample presentation from earlier in this chapter. Click the Office Button in the ribbon and choose Save As > PDF. In the Save dialog box you can specify a name and destination for the file. You can choose to optimize the file to reduce its size for e-mail, or leave it at standard quality for both print and screen. To choose different layouts, click the Options button. You can specify to print full screen slides or fit multiple slides to the page by choosing Handouts. When you've finished modifying your options, click OK to close the Options window. You should then name the file and specify a save location (such as the desktop) and click Publish. A PDF file is created, which can now be easily shared with others via e-mail and the Web.

3. View the PDF File

If the file did not automatically open, then find it in its saved location and double-click it. The PDF translation process should have occurred quickly and generated a small file that is very compatible. This file can now be shared with Windows, Mac, Linux, and multiple mobile computing platforms. When finished viewing, close the document and return to PowerPoint.

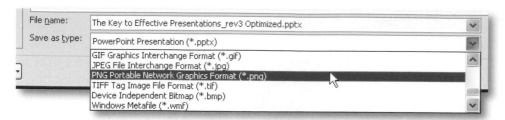

4. Choose to Save Each Slide as a Still Graphic

PowerPoint can export each slide as a still graphic. This can be very useful for those working with page layout software (like Quark Xpress or Adobe InDesign) or video editing tools (like Apple Final Cut Pro or Adobe Premiere Pro). PowerPoint supports seven different graphic formats, including the versatile JPEG and PNG formats. To save a series of still graphics, click the Office Button and choose Save As > Other Formats. Near the bottom of the Save dialog box is a Save as type drop-down menu. You can pick the file format you need (such as TIFF for printing), specify a location for the files, and click Save. PowerPoint then gives you three options: export Every Slide, Current Slide Only, or Cancel. For this example, choose Current Slide Only to write the file. ▥

INSIGHT

Which Format Do I Want? Power-Point offers several graphic formats. Here are some of the more useful choices:

- *JPG*—good for e-mailing to clients or posting to the Internet
- *PNG*—a newer format that is well suited for Web and multimedia uses
- *TIF*—best for printing
- *EMF*—preserves vectors within a slide, which is good for making enlargements

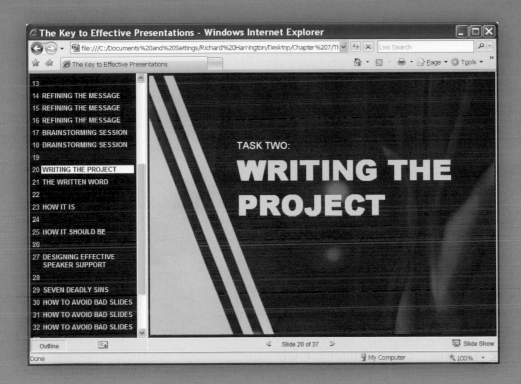

Publishing a Web Page

Placing a Presentation Online is Useful for Web Conferences and Client Reviews

1. Save the Presentation

Before you can create a Web page, you'll need to have a presentation open with no unsaved changes. You can use the same project file from earlier in the chapter, just be sure to save any changes (Ctrl+S).

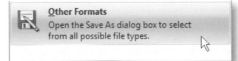

2. Use the Save As Command

In order to turn a presentation into a Web page, click the Office Button and choose Save As > Other Formats. Next specify a location to save the files to. This can be to a Web directory (such as a Web site) or to a local folder that can be transferred later to a Web server. For now, target your desktop to hold the page files.

T I P

What Is Mime HTML? This is a convenient way to embed all of the Web content into a single page. This works well for e-mail, but the recipient must use newer versions of Internet Explorer or Opera to view the file.

3. Choose a Format for the Web Archive

PowerPoint gives you two choices from the Save as type list. The first, Single File Web Page will create a Mime HTML formatted file.

The second option, Web Page, will create a folder and place all of the Web content into it. This folder can be uploaded to a server or turned into a Zip archive in order to e-mail. This option is more compatible with both Mac and PC Web browsers. Choose the Web Page option from the Save as type list.

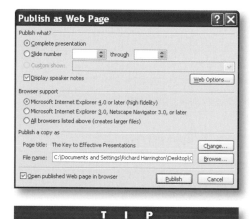

T I P

More Page Views. To increase browser compatibility, choose All browsers from the Browser support list.

4. Specify Publish Settings

Click the Publish button to specify options in the Publish as Web Page dialog box. You can modify several options that affect what your audience will see.

- Specify which slides you want to publish in the Publish what? section.

- Enable or disable speaker notes with the Display speaker notes check box.

- Modify additional properties by click Web Options. Here you can specify page color as well as image size.

- Specify which Web browser support you'd like.

- Click Browse to change the path to where you'd like to save files.

T I P

Maximum Performance. If you want to get the best results, the PowerPoint Web page looks best when viewed in Internet Explorer. In fact, several options that give you advanced controls, like an outline view and full-screen mode, are available.

5. Save the Page

Click Publish to write the Web page. PowerPoint may take a few minutes to write the file (larger presentation files will take longer). PowerPoint will create the Web page archive and place all of the files into a folder. ▦

Index

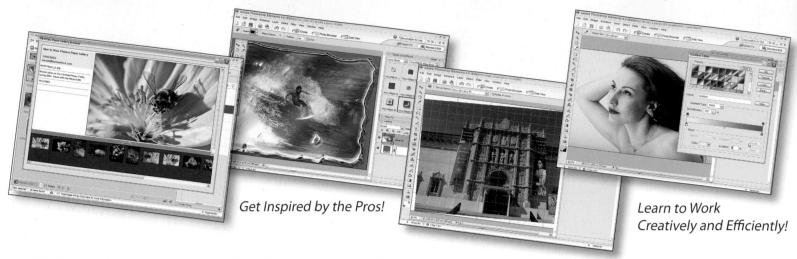

Get Inspired by the Pros!

Learn to Work Creatively and Efficiently!

You've read the book. Now see the movies!